THE
SOUS
VIDE
KITCHEN

CHRISTINA WYLIE

THE SOUS VIDE KITCHEN

Techniques, Ideas, and More Than
100 Recipes to Cook at Home

VOYAGEUR
PRESS

Quarto is the authority on a wide range of topics.
Quarto educates, entertains and enriches the lives of
our readers—enthusiasts and lovers of hands-on living.
www.quartoknows.com

© 2017 Quarto Publishing Group USA Inc.
Text and photography © 2017 Christina Wylie

First published in 2017 by Motorbooks, an imprint of The Quarto Group,
401 Second Avenue North, Suite 310, Minneapolis, MN 55401 USA.
Telephone: (612) 344-8100 Fax: (612) 344-8692

quartoknows.com
Visit our blogs at quartoknows.com

Voyageur Press titles titles are also available at discounts in bulk quantity
for industrial or sales-promotional use. For details contact the Special Sales
Manager by email at specialsales@quarto.com or by mail at The Quarto
Group, 401 Second Avenue North, Suite 310, Minneapolis, MN 55401 USA.

10 9 8 7 6 5 4 3 2 1

ISBN: 978-0-7603-5203-8

On file with Library of Congress

Acquiring Editor: Thom O'Hearn
Project Manager: Caitlin Fultz
Art Director: James Kegley
Cover Designer: Faceout Studios
Page Designer: Lauren Vajda
Layout: Amy Sly

Cover photography: Elisabeth Coelfen/Shutterstock

Printed in China

MIX
Paper from
responsible sources
FSC® C016973

CONTENTS

CHAPTER 1

THE BASICS

WHAT IS SOUS VIDE?

Juicy steaks, tender ribs, and succulent salmon are what sous vide is all about. It's a cooking method that gives you unprecedented control so that you get fantastic results, time and time again.

The literal translation of the French words *sous vide* is "under vacuum," referring to the fact that food is vacuum-sealed before it is cooked. While the vacuum-sealing aspect is important for a number of reasons, sous vide is about more than that. Primarily, it's about cooking with extreme precision when it comes to temperature.

Thomas Keller, in his classic sous vide book *Under Pressure*, says that heat is the most important ingredient in cooking but also the one that's the most difficult to control or measure reliably. For years, Keller and other professional chefs have seen the appeal of sous vide's precision. Now, home cooks have started to join the revolution. To understand why sous vide is so great, let's compare it to a few traditional cooking methods.

When pan searing a steak, high heat is applied to the surface of the steak, cooking it from the outside in. The problem is that when the center of the steak is perfectly cooked (say, medium rare), you have a ring of overcooked, gray-colored meat around the perimeter; this is referred to as the "gray band." With sous vide, you're cooking at lower temperatures, meaning you can get steak medium rare from edge to edge, and then simply sear it at a smoking hot temperature at the very end to char the surface. The result is perfectly medium-rare meat throughout, and a beautifully charred surface—no gray band.

Oven cooking presents similar drawbacks to the pan. Let's say you're cooking a rack of lamb to medium rare (130°F/54°C). You'd set your oven to a higher temperature (perhaps 350°F/177°C) and then take the lamb out of the oven when enough of the heat has penetrated the lamb so that the outside is nicely browned and the middle has just the right amount of pinkness. However, because the oven air temperature is greater than the desired internal temperature of the lamb, if you leave the lamb in there for too long, or your oven isn't perfectly calibrated, the lamb will overcook. This does not happen with sous vide; if you set a water bath to 130°F/54°C, the lamb will never go above 130°F/54°C.

This brings us back to the benefits of vacuum sealing. When cooking in the oven, moisture is constantly evaporating into the surrounding air. If you did try to cook that lamb slowly at 130°F/54°C in a traditional oven, you'd end up with something more like lamb jerky! Vacuum sealing prevents this loss of moisture with sous vide cooking.

You may now be thinking that sous vide is a lot like a slow cooker. While the two cooking methods do share similarities, sous vide has a leg up over slow cooking as well. Slow cookers help meat retain moisture, but they don't retain all the moisture of sous vide. With a slow cooker, moisture is not necessarily contained within the meat.

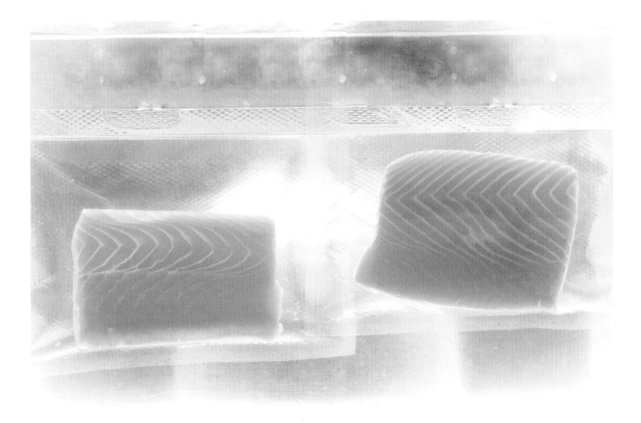

Digging a little deeper, some cuts of meat, such as brisket, become tender when cooked for long periods of time because the collagen (the connective tissue that holds muscle fibers, bones, and fat together) breaks down. This is the effect you get with traditional methods of slow cooking, such as using a slow cooker, smoking, or a long, covered bake in the oven. At the end of a traditional slow cooking, meat may be very tender, but it will also have darkened. This isn't necessarily a bad thing (think of pulled pork, for example), but the point is that you don't have the option of slow-cooked meat that's still pink in the middle. With sous vide, you can break down collagen over time *and* the meat can stay pink in the middle. This

is due to the lower temperatures that you can lock in and hold food at with sous vide.

It's not all about slow cooking, though. In addition to being great for tough meats, sous vide allows you to cook delicate foods, which require shorter and more precise cooking times. You can perfectly cook even the most delicate of fish. You can cook vegetables that still have their crunch and bright colors. When's the last time you saw a slow cooker do that?

It's worth making clear that while sous vide does have many benefits, it doesn't replace traditional cooking methods—it complements them. Some foods are ready to eat straight away after sous vide cooking, but many require a finishing method. This is because while sous vide does a fantastic job of getting the inside of foods to the optimum temperature, it doesn't offer high heat—which you need for caramelization and char. This is when cooking methods such as pan searing and barbecuing come in handy.

Thus, for many cuts of meat, sous vide cooking is the first step in a two-step process: you use sous vide to cook the interior of your food to perfection, and then use a high-heat finishing method for the surface. The combined effect is one that's greater than the sum of its parts!

Before you let two steps put you off, consider this: with sous vide you don't need to babysit your food, monitoring its progress, and you finish with intense high heat for as short a time as possible, meaning the active cooking time is actually only a couple of minutes! So if you cook sous vide and finish in a pan, your active cooking time will be shorter than if you'd cooked in a pan from start to finish.

While I hope sous vide will save you time and frustration in the kitchen—especially when it comes to meat—I also hope you'll fall in love with the food and the process as much as I have. Sous vide is currently the best way for home cooks to get consistent, restaurant-quality food without painful trial and error. And it offers unique tastes and textures simply not available with other cooking methods. So what are you waiting for? Let's get cooking!

EQUIPMENT BASICS

These days, you don't need much to get started with sous vide. Sous vide machines have come down greatly in price, making them very accessible to the home cook. The immersion-style models are adaptable as well; they can be used with a pot you already own. Most foods can be cooked sous vide using the displacement method (see page 14), but ideally you'll want a vacuum sealer because the seal created by the displacement method just isn't the same. Still, vacuum sealers are also becoming more affordable by the day. You may even find a good deal on a gently used machine.

Other than a sous vide device and a vacuum sealer, you probably already have everything you need. You can buy dedicated containers to go with an immersion sous vide machine, but they're not necessary unless you're trying to cook a lot of food at one time; generally speaking, a pot that you use to boil pasta in will suffice.

As far as finishing dishes goes, if you own a cast-iron pan or a good grill, you're pretty much sorted. The only fun toy you might seriously consider from the start is a blowtorch. It may not be considered an essential for many, but I use it so often that I consider it indispensable!

In short, here's my essential equipment list:

1. A sous vide machine (see below)

2. A vacuum sealer (see page 13)

3. A cast-iron pan (see page 31) or good barbecue grill (see page 35)

4. A blowtorch (recommended but ultimately optional, see page 33)

Sous Vide Machines

The two main types of sous vide machine are immersion circulators and water ovens. Although both are great, there are some differences. I've outlined the key differences, as well as the pros and cons, below.

Personally, I have both types of machines at home and alternate between them, sometimes preferring one more than another for different reasons. When I'm doing a lot of sous vide cooking, I tend to veer toward the water oven because I keep it out on the counter and only change the water after a few uses (it looks more attractive left out on the countertop than a pasta pot with an immersion circulator clamped to the side). When I'm cooking sous vide less frequently, the immersion circulator is handy because I can easily tuck it away in the cupboard when I'm done. It's also better if I'm cooking for a lot of people because I can adjust the sous vide water bath size. (Sometimes, I'll even have both running at the same time cooking different foods at different temperatures!)

The bottom line is I don't see any real difference in the efficacy or results of each. There's no obvious "better" option in my eyes, so feel free to pick whichever is the best fit for you and your kitchen.

IMMERSION CIRCULATOR

POPULAR IMMERSION CIRCULATOR BRANDS: *Anova, Sansaire, Nomiku, and Polyscience*
BENEFITS: Affordable, compact, flexible size for sous vide water bath
DISADVANTAGES: Can struggle with higher temperatures (over 185°F/85°C, for example)

One of the main benefits of an immersion circulator is its price; it's an increasingly affordable option and newer models are being packed with additional features. The second key benefit of an immersion circulator is its compact size; most are roughly the size of an immersion blender. To use the device, you simply attach it to the side of a large pot or other heatproof container—something like a pasta pot works great—and then fill the pot with water. You set the temperature on the machine to the temperature you want the water to be, and it will heat to precisely that temperature while circulating the water to keep it a uniform temperature throughout the sous vide water bath.

You'll have great freedom with the size of your sous vide water bath when using an immersion circulator. You can use a small pot and quickly get to temperature for a steak for one, or use a large plastic tub and cook for a party of twelve.

One potential downside of the immersion circulator is that it can take quite a while to heat to temperatures between 185°F/85°C and 203°F/95°C if you use a tub or pot with a large surface area of exposed water. One way to combat this issue is to cover the exposed surface with some foil to stop too much heat from escaping into the surrounding air. This method also helps to stop too much water from evaporating, which can happen when cooking at a high temperature for a long time. On that note, when cooking at high temperatures for a long time with an immersion circulator, be aware that you will have to top up the water intermittently so the water level does not get too low.

WATER OVEN

POPULAR WATER OVEN BRANDS: *SousVide Supreme, Gourmia, and VonShef*
BENEFITS: Handles higher temperatures better than immersion circulators
DISADVANTAGES: Bulky and more difficult to fill, drain, and store

The other common type of sous vide machine is a water oven. It looks and operates in a similar way to a rice cooker or slow cooker. You fill the water oven with water, set the temperature on the console, and then put the lid on while it heats. Because a water oven has a lid, it keeps the heat in the sous vide water bath better than an immersion circulator does, and thus speeds heating time and stops water from evaporating during the cooking process (which can be a problem when cooking at high temperatures for long periods of time).

The main downside of these machines is their bulkiness. It's not the sort of machine that you'd want to take out and put away on a daily basis, so for many it ends up being a permanent fixture on the countertop. However, many people find them more attractive than a pot with an immersion circulator clipped to the side, and so they don't mind having one on their kitchen counter as a permanent or semi permanent fixture. In short, the more you use sous vide, the more a water oven makes sense.

The other downside is more of an inconvenience: water ovens are not quite as easy to clean or drain as a pot. With an immersion circulator, you simply unclip the machine from the tub or pot, and then you can pour the water out into the sink. With a water oven, you need to unplug the machine and bring the whole thing over to the sink to tip the water out and clean inside it. Because you can't dunk the machine into a wet sink, ensuring that you clean the inside properly without getting water on any electrical elements can be tricky! It's not a huge inconvenience, but it can be slightly awkward depending on how bulky the machine is and how small your sink is.

Vacuum Sealer

Since sous vide literally means "under vacuum," it seems like we should start this section with vacuum sealing! While it may seem a bit over the top to the average home cook, vacuum sealing isn't anywhere near as high-tech as it sounds. Although you can cook many foods sous vide

without vacuum sealing (we'll discuss the alternative next), vacuum sealing is essential when you need to ensure even contact between the water bath and the item you're cooking.

Because air is less conductive than water, a good vacuum seal ensures you have the most efficient transfer of heat. When all of the air has been sucked out of the bag and the bag is sealed, your food is in direct contact with the bag on all sides, and when you submerge it into the sous vide water bath, the bag is in direct contact with the water. This allows for more even and efficient cooking than when you have air getting in the way.

To get started, all you need is your sous vide machine, a vacuum sealer, vacuum sealer bags, and whatever you're cooking. From there, it's just two easy steps. Place the food in the center of a bag and line up the open end of the bag with the sealing mechanism on the machine. Then select the appropriate setting (the standard dry setting, or a wet setting if you've used marinade, for example) and let the machine take it from there. The vacuum sealer will suck the air out of the bag and finish by melting the two sides of the bag together to create a seal.

One weakness of your standard vacuum sealer is that you can't seal bags containing liquids, because they get sucked out of the bag along with the air. The displacement method or a chamber vacuum sealer (see page 15) solves this problem. Alternatively, you can freeze your marinade before sealing it in the bag, but the cooler temperature of the frozen marinade will affect cooking time.

Vacuum sealers are very handy. In addition to being useful for sous vide cooking, vacuum sealing is a great way to save food while maintaining its best quality—and it helps you save room in the fridge or freezer. However, vacuum sealers aren't all that cheap. If you want to save money, or if you just don't want to buy one, you can get by for the most part—and for many of the recipes in this book—with the displacement method.

The Displacement Method

The displacement method is the main alternative to a vacuum sealer. Sometimes you'll want to use the displacement method in the place of a vacuum sealer even if you do have one; mainly when there's liquid in the bag, or if the food you're cooking is very delicate. I find that with even a few tablespoons of liquid in the bag, some gets sucked into the collection tray when vacuum sealing. This is particularly annoying if you've lovingly made a complex cooking sauce! The displacement method is also handy when you're cooking things like delicate fish and burger patties, which can get squashed and be left with print marks from the bag after being sealed with the more aggressive vacuum sealer.

For the displacement method, you'll need your sous vide machine, a resealable plastic bag (such as a zipper-top bag), some binder clips, whatever you're cooking, and a liquid (depending on the recipe this might be oil, butter, stock, sauce, or something else).

To get started, place the food you're cooking in the bottom of the resealable bag with enough liquid to just cover the food when you hold the

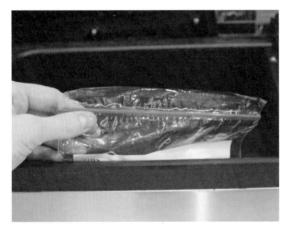

bag up in the air. The purpose of the liquid is to fill in any gaps of air that you would have had around the food due to the seal not being as tight with the displacement method as it is with a vacuum sealer. Zip the seal almost all the way, leaving a portion open for the air to be expelled through. Submerge the bag in the sous vide water bath and allow the air to be pushed out of the bag; it will be displaced by the water. Finally, when the bottom of the zip seal at the top of the bag reaches the surface of the water, zip up the remaining portion of the seal and clip the bag to the edge of your sous vide water bath with binder clips.

Although using a vacuum sealer undoubtedly creates a tighter seal around your food item, the displacement method is certainly very useful, and I don't notice a difference in quality when cooking foods in a liquid.

THE CHAMBER VACUUM SEALER

Although many vacuum sealers do have a wet setting, they are still not ideal for very saucy dishes. If you've used one before, you'll have noticed some of your prized marinade being sucked out of the top of the bag and into the collection tray. In situations like this, a chamber vacuum sealer is very handy. A chamber sealer uses a powerful vacuum pump to instantaneously suck the air out in all directions.

To be clear, a chamber vacuum sealer isn't one of the cheapest of kitchen appliances. In fact, most of them cost substantially more than the average sous vide machine that's designed for home use! For this reason, most people use either a conventional vacuum sealer or the displacement method. However, for those passionate gadget lovers or for anyone lucky enough to snag a deal on one of these, it's definitely worth a mention.

All about Bags and Sealing for Sous Vide

As you might expect, you can't use any old plastic bags for vacuum sealing; you need to buy special bags that will work with your machine. Generally, vacuum sealer bags are made from a strong plastic because they are placed under the heated strip on the sealer, which melts the bags to form a seal. It never hurts to read up on the bags you're using, but just about all vacuum-seal bags these days are BPA free and suitable for sous vide cooking.

The most commonly used bags for sealing with the displacement method are the standard resealable zipper storage bags that you see all the time at the grocery store, and probably have in a drawer at home already. You're not looking for anything fancy here, though you do need to ensure that they are the ones that are suitable for freezing, as these are slightly thicker than some others. Again, these days most manufacturers' bags are BPA free and free of other known plastics that are not safe for food, in particular if they're designed specifically for food! Still, it never hurts to read up on your bags, especially if you're ordering a lesser-known brand online. The only other thing to be aware of with resealable bags is that the shape of the bags can vary. Some have pleats in the bottom that unfold to form a flat base; you don't want those because they stop you from forming a good seal around the food.

Generally speaking, you don't want to put too many things into one bag at a time, usually around one or two items per bag, depending on the size of the bag and the item, of course. There are exceptions, such as shrimp, which you can lay flat in a single layer in a resealable bag using the displacement method, or lay flat in many layers if vacuum sealing. The reason you'd only line a single layer of shrimp along the bottom of the bag when using the displacement method is that otherwise they can fall onto each other and some edges won't be in contact with the bag anymore, resulting in unevenly cooked shrimp. No matter what you're cooking, the goal is for all of edges, or at least all of the largest edges of each piece of food in the bag to be touching the bag (or the surrounding liquid in the bag), which in turn is in direct contact with the water when submerged in a sous vide water bath. This ensures even heat transfer from the water to the food, and thus uniform sous vide cooking resulting in perfectly cooked food.

SOUS VIDE TUTORIALS

Once you have the basic equipment, it's time to get cooking! In the tutorials on the pages that follow, I've outlined the key stages of sous vide cooking as well as how to cook some of the most popular foods for sous vide: by the end, you'll be able to cook deliciously gooey sous vide eggs, a perfect sous vide steak, and even torch like a boss!

An Overview of Times and Temperatures

When dealing with different foods, it's helpful to know what you're hoping to achieve by cooking them sous vide, because what each gains from sous vide cooking is not the same.

Tougher cuts benefit from longer cooking times because the process breaks down tough collagen and tenderizes the meat. So ribs, for example, are brought to the optimum temperature and are held at this temperature for a long period of time. You also have a lot more flexibility with the cooking times for red meat, generally speaking, than foods like fish or eggs. With tough cuts like ribs or a brisket, you can go an hour or more over the allocated cooking time with very little change in texture. The same works in reverse: if you're planning to barbecue my 48-Hour Beef Ribs, for example (recipe page 75), and you start cooking at 6 p.m. on Wednesday, don't worry if you have to take it out at 4 p.m. Friday to whack on the barbecue for your hungry guests—they will still be insanely tender and a real showstopper.

Vegetables, fish, and eggs, on the other hand, can be quite delicate. Generally speaking, you only want to get them to their optimum temperature, and then remove them from the sous vide water bath before they start to degrade—eggs can overcook, fish can become mushy, and vegetables will lose their crunch. Chicken only needs to be brought to optimum temperature before it's removed from the sous vide water bath, but you do have more leeway with it in that you can leave it in for a little longer without a decline in quality. I wouldn't recommend going more than an hour or so over; otherwise, it can become mushy.

It's also worth mentioning that there is no one perfect temperature for each type of food, as was once thought in the early days of sous vide. There are certainly some optimum temperatures for attaining particular doneness: for example, a 129°F/54°C medium-rare steak. However, there is a lot more variation than pioneers initially thought, and that's why you'll find lots of conflicting information out there in terms of times and temperatures. Still, it all comes down to the doneness and the textural quality that *you* want in that particular food. What I've provided on the following pages are my tried-and-tested times and temperatures, which I know yield excellent results. I recommend using them as a baseline and then experimenting from there if you find a particular dish underdone or overdone for your liking.

Note: Ideally, food should be taken out of the fridge to sit on the countertop for 20 to 30 minutes before sous vide cooking to allow it to come to room temperature.

MEAT

- Steak (about 1½ inches thick): 129°F/54°C, 2 hours (medium rare)
- Hamburger: 130°F/54°C, 1½ hours (medium)
- Beef brisket: 135°F/57°C, 72 hours (medium, tender)
- Beef ribs: 158/70°C, 48 hours (tender, falling off bone)
- Beef rib roast: 140°F/60°C, 48 hours
- Lamb rack: 130°F/54°C, 2½ hours (medium rare)

- Lamb shoulder: 140°F/60°C, 24 hours (tender, shreds easily but still slightly pink)
- Pork loin: 136°F/58°C, 2 hours (just done, still some pinkness)
- Pork belly: 158°F/70°C, 24 hours (moist and holds shape, but can be shredded)
- Pulled pork shoulder: 158°F/70°C, 24 hours (tender, shreds easily)
- Pulled beef: 185°F/85°C, 24 hours (tender, shreds easily)
- Pork ribs: 158°F/70°C, 24 hours (tender, falling off bone)

POULTRY

- Chicken breast (light meat): 140°F/60°C, 1¼ hours
- Chicken thigh/leg (dark meat): 150°F/66°C, 2 hours
- Duck breast: 135°F/57°C, 2 hours (medium rare)
- Duck leg: 167°F/75°C, 10 hours (tender, well done, shreds easily)

FISH AND SEAFOOD

- Salmon: 122°F/50°C, 20 minutes (medium rare, silky, moist)
- White fish: 131°F/55°C, 30 minutes (silky, moist)
- Tuna steak: 104°F/40°C, 1 hour (rare)
- Shrimp, small to medium size: 135°F/57°C, 15 minutes
- Calamari/squid: 136°F/58°C, 1½ hours

- Octopus: 171°F/77°C, 7 hours
- Lobster tails: 133°F/56°C, 15 minutes
- Lobster claws: 140°F/60°C, 15 minutes
- Crab: 154°F/68°C, 45 minutes
  (steam above the water)

EGGS

Note: Eggs must start at room temperature. If your eggs are refrigerated, take them out 30 minutes before beginning sous vide cooking.

- "Poached" in shell: 147°F/64°C, 45 minutes
  (uniform gooey texture)
- "Poached" in shell: 167°F/75°C, 13 minutes
  (softer middle, harder white)
- Hard-boiled eggs: 170°F/77°C, 1 hour
- Scrambled eggs: 167°F/75°C, 30 minutes
- Gooey yolks: 144°F/62°C, 1 hour

INFUSIONS

- Infusing oils: 167°F/75°C, 3 hours
- Infusing butter: 167°F/75°C, 1 to 3 hours
- Infusing spirits: 135°F/57°C, 2 to 5 hours
- Infusing wine: 156°F/69°C, 3 hours
- Infusing cider: 156°F/69°C, 2 hours
- Infusing olives: 185°F/85°C, 4 hours

Eggs

Along with steak, sous vide eggs are one of the foods that have been integral in sparking a wider interest in sous vide in recent years. It's easy to see why. When cooked correctly, sous vide eggs have a magical gooey texture that you simply can't get with conventional cooking methods. But be warned—they are not easy to get out of the shell!

Although the general idea of sous vide is that it makes cooking food to perfection somewhat foolproof, there is still technique involved for things like sous vide eggs. First, unlike a lot of sous vide foods—in particular, red meats—eggs are quite time sensitive. If you don't cook them for long enough, they come out too runny and are almost impossible to get out of the shell in one piece. Leave them in too long, on the other hand, and you'll just have hard-boiled eggs. When you get them right, the result is an almost uniform viscous texture throughout, and a yolk that oozes when pierced as opposed to spilling all over the plate.

There are a few different temperatures that people use for sous vide eggs. You'll generally find they are somewhere between the ranges of 145°F/63°C and 167°F/75°C. The main difference between the temperatures is the level of doneness of the white. With a higher temperature, the white will be slightly harder— closer to your typical boiled or poached egg texture—while with lower temperatures the white and yolk will be a more uniform consistency. To really get the most of this unique texture, I recommend going for 147°F/64°C for 45 minutes.

STARTING TIMES AND TEMPERATURES

It's imperative that eggs be at room temperature before you begin to cook them sous vide following the temperature guidelines in this book. If you put them straight into the sous vide water bath from the fridge, or even after 10 minutes, you may end up with runny, undercooked eggs. Also, if the whites are not set enough, it's almost impossible to get the egg out of the shell in one piece. It takes around 30 minutes for eggs to get to room temperature, so just take them out a bit early, as you start to set up your water bath.

COOKING SOUS VIDE EGGS

To begin, gently lower the room-temperature eggs into a sous vide water bath preheated to the desired temperature (see the egg doneness times on page 19). I recommend using a ladle, because if you simply drop them in the shells can easily crack. When the eggs have finished cooking sous vide, fish them out of the water bath with a ladle or slotted spoon and transfer them to a bowl of warm water.

PEELING SOFT SOUS VIDE EGGS

The easiest way to peel soft sous vide eggs is while they're submerged in warm water (for hard-boiled eggs, on the other hand, I recommend peeling under running water). The most important thing to mention about this process is not to rush it! Take one egg at a time out of the water, knock the smaller end against a hard surface to crack it, and then submerge the egg back in the bowl of warm water. Gently peel away enough of the shell so that the egg can slip out of the shell and into your hand.

Don't be concerned about some of the egg white coming away from the egg into the water—this is just the outer white membrane. Allow this to fall away into the water until you're left with a clean, smooth egg.

Still cradling the egg, lift your hand out of the water and allow the excess water to drain off the egg through your fingers. Very carefully transfer the egg to the serving dish, slice of toast, or whatever you're serving it on. Take care when transferring because they are really quite delicate! Repeat the process with the rest of the eggs.

Steak

Many people are drawn to sous vide after seeing photos of perfectly cooked sous vide steaks: edge-to-edge medium rare, with none of that dreaded gray band. The good news is that what you've heard is true! Sous vide gives you the ability to cook steaks to perfection, every time. Precision cooking takes the guesswork out of the equation, allowing you to take a more relaxed "set and forget" attitude, knowing that when the buzzer on your machine sounds you'll have a tender, perfectly cooked steak. All you'll need to do at that point is sear it very quickly and serve. Having said that, another benefit of cooking steak sous vide is that you don't have to panic and get it out of the water bath straight away when it's finished; you can leave it in for even an hour over, and it will still be great. In fact, if your steak is particularly tough, I'd recommend a longer cooking time (more on time below).

Note: While traditional cooking techniques may advocate marinades for steak, with sous vide it's not necessary. If you do want to add something to the bag, a small splash of olive oil or a pat of butter and some herbs will suffice.

The guide that follows is what I've found works best for cooking a sous vide steak. Please bear in mind that I have simplified a process that can be tailored to a variety of specifications. The reason for this is to give you a clear set of parameters that yield great results, and from which you can make your modifications. In short, my perfect sous vide steak looks like this:

- Temperature: 130°F/54°C (yields medium rare)
- Time: 2 hours
- Thickness of steak: 1½ to 2 inches
- Finishing methods: pan sear with blowtorch

The main considerations we'll run through in the guide are the three Ts: temperature, time, and thickness. By paying attention to these three variables, you will get a perfectly cooked sous vide steak every time and the only part you'll need to practice will be finishing it over high heat (with a pan, on the barbecue, or with a blowtorch).

TEMPERATURE

The temperature you cook your steak at is very important because a few degrees can turn a steak from one doneness level to another. In this book, assuming you keep the time and thickness variables consistent as outlined on the following pages, you'll always shoot for the following temperatures:

- Rare: 120°F/49°C

- Medium rare: 130°F/54°C
- Medium: 135°F/57°C
- Medium well: 145°F/63°C
- Well done: 156°F/69°C+

While the temperatures above do go all the way up to well done, there's little gain in using sous vide as a method of cooking for a well-done steak. Most restaurants tend to recommend steaks cooked to medium rare, and that's what you'll find throughout this book by default. That said, everybody has their preferences and it is possible to cook a "perfect" well-done steak with sous vide. It's also much easier to hit medium and medium well without getting that tough band of meat around the outside that you'd get cooking with traditional methods.

Note: If you or a friend really wants a well-done steak that's still juicy, try cooking a fattier cut of meat with lots of marbling. You may need to cook it a bit longer to get it super tender.

TIME

Another key variable with sous vide cooking is time. In this book, I recommend cooking for 2 hours for all doneness levels while only adjusting cooking temperature. While having one set time for all temperatures may seem odd, it's the safest place to start. In practice, anywhere between 45 minutes to 3 hours is acceptable for most steaks. The main things that affect cooking time are how thick the steak is, what cut it is, how tough it is, and how long you have to prepare your meal.

For most cuts, the middle ground of 2 hours is the best place to start. It's a length of time that ensures a 1½- to 2-inch steak will have definitely reached the temperature that the sous vide machine is set to, and it will also have been held at that temperature long enough to allow for some collagen breakdown to take place to increase tenderness. Yet it doesn't let the steak stay in so long that excess collagen breaks down and the steak becomes mushy. If your steak is particularly thick, or very tough, it may benefit from a longer cooking time, perhaps 2½ to 3 hours. As a rule, I don't recommend cooking steak for longer than 4 hours; otherwise, it can become mushy. It's also worth remembering that longer cooking times can result in more moisture loss.

THICKNESS

Naturally, the thickness of the steak affects the cooking time—thicker steaks will need longer than thinner ones. I recommend reasonably thick steaks for sous vide, 1½ to 2 inches. Although you can use thinner cuts of meat, you won't get to enjoy the benefit of sous vide steak nearly as

much. After you finish the steak over high heat, you'll have far less of the perfectly cooked meat to enjoy. With a thicker cut of steak, you can get lots of tender steak inside a satisfyingly charred crust. Yes, this thickness does mean you'll have quite a large steak with some cuts! But if you want to really maximize the benefits of sous vide, a thick steak is the way to go. Share if you must!

FINISHING METHODS

After you're done cooking sous vide, but before you finish the steak, it's time to season the meat. Personally, I like to season my steaks after sous vide cooking to avoid any potential brining from long cooking times with salt. By seasoning just before finishing, I find that I get all of the tenderness and uniform doneness from sous vide cooking with all of the flavor and surface texture benefits of seasoning when it's applied right before high-heat cooking methods.

Although by no means an exhaustive list, the two methods that are most commonly used to finish sous vide steak are in a pan or on a barbecue; both of which can be complemented with a blast from a blowtorch. The most important thing to consider is that, whichever method you choose, you're using a heat source that's really, really hot. So if it's a pan, for example, you want it smoking hot before you let your steak anywhere near it.

- For more on finishing in the pan, see pages 31 to 33.
- For more on finishing on the barbecue, see page 35.
- For more on finishing with a blowtorch, see pages 33 to 35.

Chicken

Chicken, and in particular chicken breasts, are often dry and tough when cooked conventionally

to food-safe temperatures. Of course, this is not an indication of the chicken itself being tough (if that were the case, it would benefit from a long cook at a low temperature to tenderize it). Rather, it's an indication that the chicken is overcooked: too much moisture has left the chicken during cooking. Therefore, in most cases when cooking chicken sous vide, you should simply bring chicken to the optimum temperature and then remove it from the water bath. I recommend cooking at 140°F/60°C for 1 hour 15 minutes for chicken breast/light meat and 150°F/66°C for 2 hours for dark meat. Additionally, I don't recommend leaving chicken in the bath for longer than an hour over its ideal cooking time or it can become mushy.

Shellfish

Sous vide meat may get a lot of attention, but sous vide seafood can be just as impressive. While meat often benefits greatly from lengthy cooking times to break down the tough fibers, the main advantage with fish is the temperature precision. Because seafood is so easy to overcook, being super-accurate with temperatures is key. This is something that's difficult for many home cooks. Even if you're experienced, it only takes one mistake to ruin even the best the ocean has to offer. In addition, when you cook from the outside in (as you do in a skillet or cooking in the oven) you will inevitably have some flesh that becomes overcooked while the middle reaches the proper temperature.

Shellfish that work well with sous vide:
- Lobster is wonderful sous vide— see below for more information.
- Octopus and squid are both winners as well. You can get them nice and tender without overcooking. (See page 167 for an octopus recipe.)
- Shrimp are another perfect candidate, though small to medium shrimp work better. Large shrimp often get too mushy.

Don't bother cooking these shellfish sous vide:
- Oysters, in my opinion, are best raw. There may be a recipe or two where you can experiment with oysters and sous vide, but it will be the exception rather than the rule.
- Scallops are another one to skip. Since you don't want or need to cook the interiors completely, traditional cooking methods are the way to go.
- Clams and mussels have such a small amount of meat trapped inside their shells that there's really not much to gain.

LOBSTER

There are differing opinions when it comes to the perfect temperature for sous vide lobster. Chefs and home cooks use everything from around 115°F/46°C to 139°F/60°C (and in terms of sous vide, that's a pretty vast difference). Yes, the battle for the perfect lobster temperature is on!

Naturally, the higher temperature you use, the more "done" the lobster will be. Many people complain that at the lower temperatures the

lobsters are too slippery, while at the higher end of the spectrum the comments are often that the meat becomes too rubbery. After much research, I believe the happy medium for lobster tails is 133°F/56°C for 15 minutes, which yields a good firmness while being in no way rubbery. Having said that, it is *my* preferred temperature. If you try that and feel that you'd like to push it more done or less done, it's your lobster!

One last piece of advice: if you'd like to keep your lobster tails flat (stop them from curling up), use the technique shown on page 24.

Due to their difference in size and meat, tails and claws have different optimum internal temperatures—much like chicken's light and dark meat. If you're not overly concerned about your lobster tails being closer to the well-done end of the scale, then you could go ahead and cook both at the higher temperature of 140°F/60°C, but for best results I tend to cook the claws separately at 140°F/60°C for 15 minutes.

Fish

Fish needs to be brought to its optimum temperature and then immediately removed from the sous vide water bath. Like chicken, fish just doesn't benefit from longer sous vide cooking times; cook it for too long and it becomes mushy. I cook all types of white fish to 131°F/55°C for 30 minutes, and salmon at 122°F/50°C for 20 minutes. (These times work well for most fish fillets around 1½ inches.)

Salmon and tuna can benefit from brining before sous vide cooking, which gives them a firmer texture and helps them retain moisture. When brined and then cooked sous vide at low temperatures, both gain a wonderfully silky smooth texture, and I'd highly recommend trying both of my recipes that use this method. The salmon is cooked at 122°F/50°C, and the tuna at 104°F/40°C. To give it a go, check out my recipe for Rare Tuna with Olive Tapenade on page 159 and Silky Salmon with Dill Crème Fraîche on page 161.

Because fish is so delicate, you need to be careful with it when you remove it from the vacuum-seal bag after sous vide cooking to ensure it doesn't break. It's also worth bearing in mind that any seasonings, such as lemon slices or thick-stemmed herbs, may leave a mark on the surface of the fish—so you might want to serve

the fish with the seasoning still on top for presentation purposes. Alternatively, you can simply season the fish after cooking sous vide.

Vegetables and Fruit

Boiling vegetables can work well if you take them out at the exact right time, but overcook them slightly and they go soft and begin to lose their color. Not only that, but you're also losing nutrients to the surrounding water—no wonder they're increasingly pale the longer you cook them. This is a consequence not only of cooking in water, but also of high, harsh temperatures. Sous vide eradicates both of these issues. You can cook them to the perfect level of doneness without exposing them to very high heat, and because they're sealed, you won't lose nutrients to the water.

Although you probably don't cook fruit as often as vegetables, the same points hold true. You're also able to precisely hit exact levels of doneness that are more difficult with conventional cooking methods like baking, and the fruit will lose fewer nutrients than it would if exposed to high temperatures. Check out my recipes for poached pears (page 236), Pear, Parmesan, and Walnut Salad (page 114), and even apple pie filling (page 239).

BEFORE SOUS VIDE

Although additional prep work before sous vide isn't necessary very often, there are a few foods and recipes that benefit from a bit of extra attention before you begin cooking. Here are a few of the main techniques you can consider.

Salt and Seasoning

Some people like to add seasoning to their food before cooking it sous vide to infuse flavor during the sous vide process. Although this does have its benefits in certain instances—and you will see it done in some recipes in this book—you need to be aware of the salt content in any seasoning or marinade, along with the length of time and temperature you're cooking at.

If you were cooking a steak in a skillet, you'd probably season it before you put it in the pan, and then maybe again after. Cooking steak sous vide, however, doesn't work like that. If you put salt on a steak before vacuum sealing it and cooking it sous vide at a low temperature for a number of hours, the salt will then begin to cure the steak. The result is a denser, pickled texture and flavor.

Thus, many people choose to season their steaks after sous vide cooking, immediately prior to a flash fry in a hot skillet to brown the outside. The same applies for anything you're cooking for long periods of time at a low temperature—think tough cuts of beef, pork, or lamb.

For fish fillets, on the other hand, you'll only be cooking them for a short amount of time. This means they can take a marinade with salt before cooking sous vide should you wish to add it (see pages 159 and 161 for an example of this). The same thing applies to vegetables that you cook at high temperatures for short periods of time; go ahead and salt them before cooking sous vide if you'd like.

Marinades

The two main purposes of a marinade are to tenderize and to infuse flavor. Let's start with the tenderizing aspect. Chicken, fish, vegetables, and the like will all be perfectly tender as soon as they reach their optimum temperature. For tougher cuts of meat, you'll already be holding them at the optimum temperature for a while in order to break down some of the tough collagen and make the meat tender. So no matter what you're cooking, the sous vide cooking will tenderize your food perfectly without a marinade.

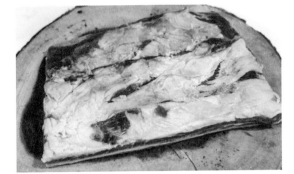

However, there's still the benefit of infusing flavors with a marinade. The only word of caution is again the salt: if you are cooking something for a good few hours at a low temperature and want to use a marinade, it should be a salt-free one. As with the seasonings, something cooked for a shorter time, about a half hour or less, can be cooked sous vide in a marinade that contains a normal amount of salt.

Dry Rubs

Dry rubs can work particularly well with meats such as beef, pork, lamb, and chicken. The most important thing to consider when using a dry rub to cook something for long periods of time at low temperatures using sous vide is—you guessed it—the salt content! You want your rub to contain little to no salt because the salt will cure/brine your food just like straight salt or a salty marinade would.

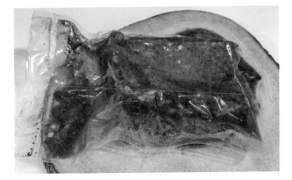

Most dry rubs will contain pepper, some kind of chile (e.g., dried chiles, chili powder, cayenne pepper, and/or paprika). Often granulated or powdered onion and/or garlic is part of the rub as

well—but be careful to check that these powders don't have salt in them when applying them before sous vide cooking. For extra flavor you can also add dried herbs (e.g., oregano, cumin, and/or coriander). You can either apply the dry rub straight to the meat or apply a thin layer of olive oil to the meat first and then the rub (this can help the rub stick to the surface of the meat). For examples of my dry rub in action, see 72-Hour Beef Brisket (page 80), Smoked Beef Ribs (page 75), and Baby Back Ribs with Bourbon Barbecue Sauce (page 73).

Brining

Okay, so we've talked about how you don't want to brine certain meats while you're cooking sous vide. While that's true as a general rule, the controlled brining of certain foods before cooking can help them turn out even better. The brine will enable the meat (or fish) to retain additional moisture during the cooking process.

A brine is essentially a saltwater solution. Some people like to fancy up their brines with sugar, lemon wedges, onion slices, garlic cloves, and the like, but the salt is what makes a brine a brine. Due to its salt content, buttermilk can also be used as a base for a brine. The amount of time you need to brine for depends on what you're brining and its size. For example, a chicken breast would need substantially less time to brine than a whole chicken. Check out these recipes for examples of foods made better with brine: Spicy Southern-Fried Chicken (page 95), 24-Hour Pork Belly with Potato Purée and Caramelized Apple (page 86), Silky Salmon with Dill Crème Fraîche

(page 161), and Rare Tuna with Olive Tapenade (page 159).

Pre-Searing

When you're trying to stop meat from going much higher than the optimum internal temperature, it may seem counterintuitive to sear it both before and after cooking. However, there are a number of benefits. Let's say you're after a perfect medium-rare steak. If you give the steak a quick flash in a skillet while it's cold, less of the meat under the surface will overcook than if you sear it while it's hot, simply because it's cooler and will take longer to reach higher temperatures; of course, you'll still need to sear it again after sous vide cooking.

The theory behind this pre-searing is that when you go to sear it again at the end, you won't have to cook it for as long because you've already begun the process. So although you do have to sear it twice, if your skillet is hot enough, the steak will actually have less of that dreaded gray band thanks to pre-searing. Although I don't often see the need to pre-sear foods like steak, I have had better results when pre-searing the skin side of foods such as skin-on duck breast and skin-on chicken breast than without pre-searing. Without pre-searing, too much of the meat under the skin gets overcooked by the time the skin is reasonably crispy. In general, though, I steer away from cooking skin-on foods sous vide as I don't think they ever get satisfyingly crispy after getting soggy through sous vide cooking. Sometimes I do cook the skin separately, as you can see in my recipe for Thyme and Garlic Chicken Thighs (page 41).

AFTER SOUS VIDE

When food comes out of a vacuum-seal bag, it's often not quite ready to serve as is. Many things that you cook sous vide will require some kind of finishing step. This is because while sous vide cooking does an excellent job of getting the interior of food to perfection, it doesn't offer much for the surface—for that you need higher temperatures. (Sous vide can't brown or caramelize.) With this in mind, here are a few of the key finishing techniques that will get your food ready to serve.

Searing

This technique is perfect for meats like steak, chicken breast, and skin-on duck breast. It's probably the simplest of the finishing techniques, but very useful. Generally speaking, sear the exterior of the food in as little time as possible. To do this, the skillet needs to be as hot as possible to minimize cooking time. Although this is not always the case, it will be true for most recipes. Also, use a cooking fat that has a high smoke point so that you can get it really hot. In other words, extra-virgin olive oil is not ideal, butter works better (with short cooking times), and high-smoke-point oils and clarified butter work

best. You get the best char with a gas burner; the electric ones just don't get hot enough, which is very disappointing when you inadvertently overcook your lovingly prepared sous vide steak because you can't get a good sear in time. The exact temperature will vary by meat. For example, you'll sear a steak for 30 seconds to 1 minute on each side in a super-hot pan; if you're rendering the thick fat of a duck breast, a slightly lower temperature is ideal so that you can render more of the fat without burning the surface of the skin that's touching the skillet.

CHOOSING YOUR PAN

First things first: you need a proper pan for searing at very high temperatures—the heavier, the better. Avoid Teflon frying pans and frying pans with other manufactured nonstick coatings as well as tin-lined copper frying pans. You do have a few options though. Here's a list of suitable pans:

- Tri-ply or All-Clad stainless steel frying pans
- Cast-iron frying pan or grill pan
- Carbon steel frying pan
- Copper frying pans

CHOOSING YOUR OIL

Once your pan is smoking hot, make sure you have oil with a high smoke point on hand, or butter. Personally, I prefer butter because it gives a lovely rich flavor as well as a darker color to the meat. However, bear in mind that you don't want to cook butter at high temperatures for too long or it will burn and become black and bitter. If you're cooking with butter in a hot pan for more than one round (i.e., you're making lots of steaks), wipe down the pan with paper towels between each piece and add new butter each time.

Note: Clarified butter, on the other hand, has a much higher smoke point, so it is great for searing at high temperatures.

With one of the lowest smoke points out there, extra-virgin olive oil is about the worst for cooking with at high temperatures, so keep that for your salads. As far as the other oils go, consider smoke point and flavor. Let's run through some of the most common suitable choices.

Suitable oils (in order of smoke point, high to low):

- Safflower oil: 510°F/265°C
- Rice bran oil: 490°F/260°C
- Light/refined olive oil: 465°F/240°C
- Soybean oil: 450°F/230°C
- Peanut oil: 450°F/230°C
- Clarified butter: 450°F/230°C
- Corn oil: 450°F/230°C
- Sunflower oil: 440°F/225°C
- Vegetable oil: 400°F to 450°F/205°C to 230°C
- Canola oil: 400°F/250°C
- Grapeseed oil: 390°F/195°C

SEAR IT

When you have an appropriate pan and your oil is at the ready, it's time to sear.

1. Place your pan on the burner and turn your burner to high.

2. Let the pan sit there until it's heated all the way through; be patient as this can take anywhere from a couple of minutes for some pans up to around 10 minutes for a thick cast-iron pan. You don't want to jump the gun or you'll end up either overcooking the meat under the surface or having a subpar char.

3. When the pan is smoking hot, add the fat that you've chosen to use (either oil or butter). Allow the oil or butter to heat for just a few seconds, and then place your food into the hot fat.

4. Sear for as little time as possible, while getting as much char on the outside as possible. Keep your pan glued to the burner and let that high heat do its thing. However, don't squash your meat against the pan with a spatula! The steam you see leaving the meat when you do that is moisture squeezed from the inside of the meat and will be gone forever.

You might be used to resting meat, but another plus point of sous vide cooking is that you don't need to leave meat to rest. If you do need it to sit around for a minute or two before serving while you put the finishing touches on the rest of the meal, keep the meat on a wire rack so you don't ruin the magnificent crust that you've just made.

The Blowtorch

A blowtorch is the ultimate high-heat tool. It will give your meat a smoky flavor in a hurry and it works particularly well with red meat. Once you've used a blowtorch, you'll see the light, and you'll discover it's also quite fun! Having

said that, always exercise caution when using a blowtorch—it's definitely not a toy.

Note: A common mistake that people make when selecting a blowtorch for finishing sous vide meats is buying a culinary torch. These small torches are good for finishing a brûlée, but they don't offer much when it comes to getting good char on the outside of a steak. The most popular torch for cooking in this manner is a small propane gas torch; however, you can also use a butane gas canister with a high-output torch head.

When your cut of meat has been cooked sous vide and you're ready to torch, place the food on a thick, heat-proof surface. Or you can torch directly in a pan or over a barbecue if you're torching as the food cooks. If you're torching afterward, a baking tray works well. You may think aluminum foil would provide a safe barrier, but it doesn't! A strong blowtorch will burn right through it.

When using a blowtorch, the surface area receiving heat at any given time is small. So the idea is to keep the blowtorch moving steadily to achieve an even sear over the entire surface. If you focus on one area at a time, you're more likely to get burnt patches and uneven charring on your meat. Make sure you don't forget the edges or fatty bits on the end of meat either. Don't hold the meat while you torch it, though. Just change the angle of the torch as needed to hit the sides when the meat is on your safe, heatproof surface. As you turn a piece of food over to torch the other side, take care to think about spots you might miss.

It's also worth noting that because it is so hot, a blowtorch is only rarely a standalone finishing method. You can use it by itself for shrimp or other small cuts of meat; however, with a steak or other larger cuts, using a blowtorch alone only hits the top layer of the surface. A blowtorch doesn't permeate deep enough to develop a satisfying crust. With those larger, thicker meats, you'll probably want to finish on a barbecue or in a pan, using a blowtorch only to augment the heat.

TOP TIPS FOR TORCHING FOOD

- Safety first! Remember that you are playing with fire (literally). Make sure your blowtorch's head is firmly attached to the gas canister before you begin, and ensure that you turn it all the way off when you're finished—you don't want gas leaking out.

- Size matters. My first torch was a tiny little kitchen torch for caramelizing crème brûlée, which although very cute, basically just tickled the steak. Get yourself a proper high-output blowtorch: the bigger, the better (within reason).

- To avoid "torch taste," make sure you turn the torch on and properly adjust the flame before you point it at the food. Before you apply it to the food, you want to ensure the flame is fully oxidizing. The telltale sign for this is a shorter flame that burns dark blue. If your flame is longer and yellow at the tip, it means it contains uncombusted hydrocarbons from the fuel, which can result in torch taste.

- Ensure you torch on a thick heat-proof surface! If you're torching in a pan, that's great. A baking tray works well, too. Aluminum foil will not work; the blowtorch will burn right through it.

- Use slow, sweeping strokes across the food, as opposed to concentrating on one small area for a long time and then moving to the next. This helps avoid burning in concentrated spots, and it helps you get a more even char across the surface.

- Remember that torching is rarely a standalone finishing method; it complements your primary finishing method.

FOODS YOU CAN TORCH

- **Shrimp:** A blowtorch can be used as a standalone finishing method.
- **Steak:** Sear in the pan or on the barbecue and torch simultaneously.
- **Ribs:** Sear in the pan or on the barbecue and torch simultaneously, or finish under the broiler and then torch afterward.
- **Brisket:** Sear in the pan or on the barbecue and torch simultaneously, or finish under the broiler and then torch afterward.
- **Desserts (crème brûlée, meringue, etc.):** Torch the surface as a standalone finishing method.

Barbecue

If you're after tender ribs with a smoky flavor using sous vide, you'll likely want to finish them on the barbecue. You get the best of both worlds: tender meat and a charred, smoky exterior! This technique doesn't just work for ribs; it's also great for brisket, sausages, burgers, and chicken, to name a few.

The key differences between cooking something on the barbecue from raw and cooking it from sous vide are the cooking time and temperature. After sous vide cooking, the food requires a shorter amount of time on the grill and also a ripping hot temperature. Again, the goal is to not overcook the center of the meat but to add some character and flavor to the surface as quickly as possible. After all, the meat is already cooked to the optimum temperature all the way

through; the grilling is just to get a different flavor and texture on the exterior.

If you're using a gas barbecue, turn it on high and close the lid for 5 to 10 minutes. If you're using a coal barbecue, light the coals and let them burn for 5 to 10 minutes. The recipes in this book will provide cooking times, but in general you're doing the exact same thing you'd do with a hot pan. You'll want just 1 minute on each side for burgers, steaks, chicken breast, sausages, and so on. Thicker cuts of meat like brisket can go longer, 2 to 2½ minutes on each side.

Note: Just because you're barbecuing doesn't mean you shouldn't use a blowtorch, too! While the food is on the barbecue, torch the side that's facing up, then repeat after you flip it. Check out my guide to torching on page 33.

BROILING/ROASTING

The oven can be a handy tool for finishing sous vide foods. As usual, the goal is to apply maximum heat to the already-cooked food in the shortest amount of time, so you want to use very high heat (such as the highest setting on the broiler). Hardy foods such as ribs, brisket, and prime rib roast work well with this type of finishing method.

CHAPTER 2
GETTING STARTED

What came first, the sous vide chicken or the sous vide egg? In this book, the first recipe will introduce you to both! Before you skip this recipe and head to the steak, hear me out. I, too, was not very excited about chicken before I started cooking sous vide. After all, when the internal temperature guidelines for "safe" chicken recommends 165°F/74°C—well above the optimal cooking temperature for chicken—biting into dry chicken is inevitable. Sous vide solves the problem, as holding poultry at 140°F/60°C for over an hour has the same effect on harmful pathogens as a short burst at 165°F/74°C. This means moist, tender chicken is also food-safe chicken!

You can find more detail on eggs on pages 19 to 20, as well as more recipes for eggs starting on page 213. However, I couldn't resist introducing eggs in the first recipe. Every little adjustment in temperature affects the resulting texture—and there are so many wonderful egg doneness levels for you to experience with sous vide. In this recipe, we'll go for nearly hard-boiled. I guarantee they will be the best you've ever had.

COBB SALAD

🌡* 140°F/60°C (CHICKEN), 170°F/77°C (EGG)

⏱ 1 HOUR 15 MINUTES (CHICKEN), 1 HOUR (EGG) | 🍴 SERVES 4

INGREDIENTS

8 eggs

2 chicken breast fillets

8 slices bacon, diced

4 heads romaine lettuce, chopped

2 tomatoes, chopped

2 avocados, peeled, pitted, and sliced

½ red onion, chopped

1 cup/113 g crumbled blue cheese

Salt and black pepper

1 teaspoon/5 g yellow mustard

RANCH DRESSING

1 cup/226 g mayonnaise

½ cup/113 g sour cream

2 teaspoons/3⅓ g finely chopped fresh chives, plus extra to garnish

1 teaspoon/5 g yellow mustard

½ teaspoon/2½ g garlic powder

Sea salt and black pepper to taste

DIRECTIONS

Preheat a sous vide water bath to 170°F/77°C.

Carefully drop the eggs into the preheated sous vide water bath with a ladle, and cook for 1 hour. When the eggs are done, remove them from the sous vide bath and separate them from their shells (see page 20 for my method). Roughly chop them and set aside if you're making the salad straight away, or cover and refrigerate if using later or the next day.

Note: Because the eggs will ideally be served cold, you don't need to cook them just before eating them, or even on the same day. You can cook them the day before and simply store them in the fridge until you want to use them. See pages 19 to 21 for a complete egg tutorial.

Preheat a sous vide water bath to 140°F/60°C.

Seal the chicken breasts in individual vacuum seal bags, or with 2 per bag, and cook in the preheated sous vide water bath for 1 hour 15 minutes.

While the chicken cooks, mix the ranch dressing ingredients in a small bowl. Then, in a medium-size bowl, combine 1 cup/240 g of the ranch dressing with an additional 1 teaspoon of yellow mustard and the chopped eggs. Cover and refrigerate the egg salad and the remaining ranch dressing.

When the chicken has finished cooking sous vide, plunge the bag into an ice bath for 5 to 10 minutes.

Meanwhile, heat a frying pan over medium heat and fry the bacon until crispy, then set the bacon aside on paper towels, discarding the grease (or saving it for another recipe!).

Cut open the vacuum seal bag and discard any liquid. Transfer the chicken to a cutting board and cut it into cubes. In a large bowl, combine the romaine, tomatoes, avocado, red onion, and blue cheese. Toss to combine.

Serve the salad on individual plates (or one large plate), topping with the chicken and scattering the bacon bits over the top. Serve the egg salad and extra ranch dressing in bowls alongside. Garnish with chopped chives, and season with salt and black pepper to taste.

A common complaint with sous vide cooking is that you can't get properly crispy skin on chicken—or fish, or most things for that matter! This is because the skin gets almost irreversibly soggy after cooking for a long time in a vacuum-sealed bag. Then, if you try to fry it while it's still attached to the meat, by the time you get the skin crispy, the meat underneath will be overcooked.

The solution is to remove the chicken skin before sous vide cooking. By doing this, I found that I was able to get the best of both worlds: crispy skin as well as moist chicken meat. This dish takes that winning combination and adds lemon, garlic, thyme, and burnt butter for an easy-to-make dish that's still creative and unique.

THYME AND GARLIC CHICKEN THIGHS

🌡 150°F/66°C | ⏱ 2 HOURS | 🍴 SERVES 4

INGREDIENTS

8 tablespoons/113 g unsalted butter, divided

12 skin-on chicken thighs, skin removed and reserved in the fridge

1 lemon, cut into wedges

8 garlic cloves, crushed

12 sprigs fresh thyme

Vegetable oil, for deep-frying

Sea salt and pepper

DIRECTIONS

Preheat a sous vide water bath to 150°F/66°C.

Heat a frying pan over high heat, and then add 6 tablespoons/ 85 g of the butter. Fry the skinless chicken thighs for 1 to 2 minutes on each side, spooning the hot butter over the chicken as it cooks, then transfer to a large bowl. Pour out the butter and wipe out the frying pan with paper towels.

Return the pan to the burner and char the lemon wedges by cooking them in the clean pan for a few minutes, then transfer the lemons to the large bowl. Melt the remaining 2 tablespoons/28 g butter in the pan and add the garlic cloves. Fry for a few minutes, until fragrant. Add the thyme and continue to fry for 10 to 30 seconds until just browned, then tip the contents of the pan into the bowl with the chicken thighs. Toss to combine.

Transfer the contents of the bowl to a large resealable plastic bag. Seal the bag using the displacement method (see page 14), clip the bag to the side of the preheated water bath, and cook for 2 hours.

Just before the chicken has finished cooking sous vide, pour 4 inches/10 cm of oil into a deep fryer or pot and heat to 400°F/200°C. Pat the reserved chicken skins dry, generously season with salt, and lay them out flat on a chopping board. Carefully lift the skin pieces up from one end and drop into the oil (this is to keep them as straight as you can, although they will still curl up a bit). Deep-fry the skins for a few minutes until they're golden and crispy, then set aside on paper towels.

Remove the chicken and seasonings from the sous vide bag, discarding any excess liquid, and arrange on a serving dish. Season with salt and pepper. Scatter the chicken skin pieces over the top and serve immediately.

This is it: the main event. Get excited because this recipe shows you how to cook a steak that is wall-to-wall medium rare—and you definitely won't see that dreaded gray band of overcooked meat once you cut into it. While you might need to practice this recipe a few times to get it truly perfect, don't be surprised if you're soon making the best steak you've had anywhere. For a bit of supplemental reading on sous vide steak, check out pages 8 and 21 to 23.

THE PERFECT STEAK

🌡* 135°F/54°C | ⏲ 2 HOURS (SEE NOTE) | 🍴 SERVES 4 TO 6

INGREDIENTS

4 steaks of your choice, approximately 1½ inches/ 4 cm thick (you can choose from rib eye, porterhouse, tenderloin, strip, hanger, flap, or skirt)

Salt and black pepper

4 tablespoons/56 g unsalted butter, divided

4 garlic cloves, peeled and halved, divided

1 bunch fresh thyme

Note: There's not a huge difference in the way you cook different cuts of steak with sous vide, but you want to adjust the sous vide time and temperature according to the thickness of your steak; a really thick steak should be cooked sous vide a bit longer, and a thinner steak doesn't need as much time.

DIRECTIONS

Preheat a sous vide water bath for the doneness level of your steak. I recommend 130°F/54°C for medium rare, but here are the other options:

DONENESS LEVEL	TEMPERATURE
RARE	120°F (49°C)
MEDIUM RARE	130°F (54°C)
MEDIUM	135°F (57°C)
MEDIUM WELL	145°F (63°C)
WELL DONE	156°F (69°C+)

Seal your steaks in individual vacuum seal bags, or 2 per bag, and cook in the preheated water bath for 2 hours.

When the steaks have finished cooking sous vide, start heating up your pan over high heat until it's smoking hot (up to 10 minutes for a cast-iron pan). While the pan is heating, remove the steaks from the bags, pat dry with paper towels, and rub a generous amount of salt and pepper onto all sides. Once the pan is hot, add 1 tablespoon of the butter, 1 of the garlic cloves, and 4 sprigs of the thyme, followed immediately by one of the steaks.

Searing a sous vide steak is very different to the process of searing a raw steak. First, when your steak comes out of the sous vide water bath, the interior meat is cooked to perfection. All you're looking to do is get some char on the outside, with minimum cooking under the surface. This is why you want to get the pan as hot as possible and cook the steak as quickly as possible. It's also important for the steak to be patted dry with paper towels before frying, as any moisture on the surface will increase the amount of frying time needed to get a good char.

Fry just until you get a good sear, around 1 to 1½ minutes on each side, and set the steak aside on a wire rack. Wipe the pan with paper towels after finishing the first steak, and repeat the process with the remaining steaks.

Note: If you want to use a blowtorch to add extra char, sear the steak for 30 seconds or so on each side. Then for the last two sets of 30 seconds, torch the side facing up while the side facing down sears in the pan. Cooking the steak for 1 minute less helps even out the extra heat added by the torch. (See pages 33 to 35 for more on this technique.)

Can't get enough of sous vide steak? This pub classic is perfect for an afternoon cookout or easy mid-week dinner. Fill a baguette with tender, perfectly cooked steak, some fried onions, and a dollop of horseradish cream and you're good to go. It's a simple yet satisfying meal that never gets old. Hosting a crowd? This is an easy recipe to double. The caramelized onions can be made ahead of time and the horseradish cream can be made the day before. You can pop the steaks in the sous vide water bath a couple of hours before you're ready to eat and hang out with your friends and family until it's time to sear and serve.

STEAK SANDWICH WITH HORSERADISH CREAM

🌡 129°F/54°C | ⏲ 2 HOURS | 🍴 SERVES 4

INGREDIENTS

Two 1½- to 2-inch/4- to 5-cm-thick steaks of your choice (rib eye, porterhouse, tenderloin, strip, hanger, flap, or skirt)

2 tablespoons/30 ml olive oil

2 white onions, thinly sliced

Salt and pepper to taste

2 tablespoons/28 g unsalted butter, divided

4 individual baguettes or mini focaccia buns

Butter lettuce leaves

1 tomato, sliced

HORSERADISH CREAM

½ cup/113 g sour cream

2 tablespoons/28 g grated fresh horseradish (or jarred if you can't find fresh)

2 teaspoons/10 g Dijon mustard

½ teaspoon/2½ ml white wine vinegar

Salt and black pepper to taste

DIRECTIONS

Preheat a sous vide water bath to 129°F/54°C.

Seal the steaks in individual vacuum seal bags and cook in the preheated water bath for 2 hours.

While the steaks cook, make the horseradish cream. Place all of the horseradish cream ingredients in a small bowl and stir well to combine. Cover and refrigerate.

With about 40 minutes left on the steaks, start caramelizing the onions. Heat the olive oil in a frying pan over low heat. Add the onions and a pinch of salt. Cook, stirring occasionally, for about 40 minutes, or until the onions are sticky and caramelized.

When the steaks have finished cooking sous vide, take them out of the bags. Pat them dry and season generously with salt and pepper. Heat a frying pan over high heat until it is smoking hot—this can take up to 10 minutes for a cast-iron pan. Add 1 tablespoon of the butter and fry the steaks one at a time for 1 to 1½ minutes on each side, until well charred. Wipe the pan with paper towels between each steak, add the remaining 1 tablespoon butter, and fry the second steak. Set the steaks aside on a cutting board. Let rest for a few minutes, and then slice very thin with a sharp knife.

Toast your bread, if you wish. Then layer up your sandwich: lettuce on the bottom, followed by tomato slices, steak slices, and finally the caramelized onions. Add the horseradish cream to taste on the top slice of bread and you're ready to serve!

The reason this recipe is suspiciously called a "stew" is because of the way it's cooked. Despite the final dish looking and tasting like a stew, the process is vastly different; the beef is cooked separately from the rest of the stew! The reason behind this is to get the best out of each part of the dish before bringing it all back together. You'll see that when combined, they create a dish that's greater than the sum of its parts. You may forever be converted to "stew."

Most people's next question is "why?" For this recipe, there are a number of reasons. First, some ingredients—garlic and salt, in particular—are not recommended for hours of cooking at low temperatures. In addition, the beef becomes tender with 8 hours of sous vide cooking, meaning there's no need for tenderizing elements to be in the bag. Flavor-wise, in the last step you cut the beef into small chunks and mix it up with the rich sauce; the tender shreds absorb all that flavor-packed goodness, so there isn't a real need to impart flavor during the sous vide process.

SLOW-COOKED BEEF "STEW"

🌡* 140°F/60°C | ⏲ 8 HOURS | 🍴 SERVES 4 TO 6

INGREDIENTS

2 tablespoons/30 ml vegetable oil

1½ to 2 pounds/680 to 910 g chuck steak

4 tablespoons/56 g unsalted butter

4 slices bacon, chopped into lardons

1 onion, julienned

5 garlic cloves, thinly sliced

18 ounces/500 g cremini mushrooms, thinly sliced (button or portobello mushrooms work well too)

1 bottle (750 ml) dry red wine

1 tablespoon/15 g beef bouillon

6 ounces/170 g tomato paste

1 can (14 ounces/400 g) diced tomatoes

2 teaspoons fresh thyme leaves, divided

2 bay leaves

1 tablespoon/15 g cornstarch mixed with 2 tablespoons water

Salt and pepper to taste

DIRECTIONS

Preheat a sous vide water bath to 140°F/60°C.

Rub the vegetable oil on the steak. Heat a frying pan over high heat until it just starts to smoke. Sear the steak for 1 to 2 minutes on each side. Transfer the steak to a large vacuum-seal bag, seal, and cook in the preheated water bath for 8 hours (if you don't have a bag that's large enough, you can chop it into two or more pieces so that it fits in the bags you have).

When the beef has finished cooking sous vide, heat a pot over medium heat. Add the butter and fry the bacon for a few minutes. Add the onion and garlic, fry for a few minutes, and then add the mushrooms and fry until tender. Pour in the bottle of dry red wine and stir in the bouillon, tomato paste, canned tomatoes, 1 teaspoon of the thyme leaves, and the bay leaves.

Cut open the vacuum-seal bag containing the sous vide beef and pour any liquids from the bag into the sauce. Re-submerge the bag containing the beef in the sous vide water bath and clip it to the edge of the pot to keep it warm. Bring the pot of stew liquid to a boil. Leave it at a rolling boil until the sauce reduces by about half, 10 to 15 minutes. Stir in the cornstarch mixture to thicken the sauce. Add salt and pepper to taste.

Take the beef out of the sous vide bag, chop it into rough chunks, and add it to the stew. Remove the bay leaves and remove the pot from the heat. Serve topped with the remaining 1 teaspoon thyme leaves.

Lasagna was the inspiration for this dish, but as you'll see there are a few key departures. In addition to it not being baked in a large dish, there's no ground beef in sight. Instead, it combines tender, slow-cooked sous vide beef with a tomato and portobello mushroom sauce. Spooned generously atop lasagna noodles, it's a grown-up version of the childhood favorite.

DECONSTRUCTED LASAGNA

♨ 185°F/85°C | ⏱ 24 HOURS | ✗ SERVES 4

INGREDIENTS

1 pound/450 g beef brisket

8 lasagna noodles

1 pound/450 g grated mozzarella

2 tablespoons/12½ g grated Parmesan

SAUCE

1 tablespoon/14 g unsalted butter

8 ounces/227 g portobello mushrooms, sliced

2 garlic cloves, crushed

1½ cans (14 ounces/300 g each) chopped tomatoes

¼ cup/65 g tomato paste

1 bay leaf

Sea salt and black pepper

½ cup/25 g fresh basil leaves, plus 1 leaf per lasagna for garnish

DIRECTIONS

Preheat a sous vide water bath to 185°F/85°C.

Seal the brisket in a vacuum-seal bag and cook in the preheated water bath for 24 hours.

When the brisket has finished cooking sous vide, make the sauce. Heat a medium-size pot over medium heat (you can leave the brisket in the water bath for now). Add the butter and fry the mushrooms until soft, 5 to 10 minutes. Add the garlic and cook for 2 minutes. Add the canned tomatoes, tomato paste, and bay leaf and cook until the sauce is bubbling, 5 to 10 minutes. Add salt and pepper to taste and decrease the heat to low. Simmer for 10 to 15 minutes to combine the flavors.

While the sauce is simmering, cook the lasagna noodles, drain, and cut them in half. Set aside.

Remove the beef from the bag and shred it with two forks. Remove the sauce from the heat, add the shredded beef and basil leaves, and stir to combine.

Turn your broiler on high and allow it to preheat. While it heats, assemble the individual lasagnas on a well-oiled baking sheet. To assemble, start by placing 4 lasagna sheets on the tray, followed by a generous sprinkle of mozzarella, then spoon on the beef and sauce. Top each with another lasagna sheet, some more mozzarella, and Parmesan. Place under the broiler for 2 to 5 minutes, or until the top is nicely browned. Remove from the broiler and carefully transfer to plates with an oiled spatula.

Cooking something for 48 hours may seem like an extraordinarily long time, and one that's almost impossible with conventional cooking methods seeing as you'd undoubtedly have to leave it unattended for periods of time—one must get one's beauty sleep, go to work, and other such daily endeavors.

In this recipe, we'll use sous vide similar to how you'd use a slow cooker. As you'd expect, after 48 hours at 143°F/62°C you'll find this lamb shank is fall-off-the-bone tender. In fact, since you'll lose far less moisture, and since the cooking time is two full days, this lamb is even better than its slow-cooked counterpart.

48-HOUR LAMB SHANK

🌡 143°F/62°C | ⏱ 48 HOURS | 🍴 SERVES 4

INGREDIENTS

4 bone-in lamb shanks

4 tablespoons/56 g unsalted butter

4 garlic cloves, thinly sliced

1 onion, julienned

7 ounces/200 g mushrooms of your choice, thinly sliced

2 teaspoons/2 g thyme leaves, plus extra leaves and whole sprigs to serve

1½ cups/350 ml dry red wine

1½ cups/350 ml tomato sauce

Salt and freshly ground black pepper

DIRECTIONS

Preheat a sous vide water bath to 143°F/62°C.

Seal the lamb shanks in vacuum-seal bags (you can either seal each shank in an individual bag, or put 2 in each bag) and cook in the preheated water bath for 48 hours.

When the lamb has finished cooking sous vide, heat a frying pan over medium heat. (You can leave the lamb in the water bath while you prepare the sauce.) Add the butter and fry the garlic and onion for a few minutes until the onions are tender and the butter begins to brown. Add the mushrooms and thyme. Cut open the vacuum-seal bag and pour the juices from the bag into the frying pan. Add the red wine and tomato sauce and bring to a boil to burn off the alcohol, then immediately decrease the heat to maintain a simmer.

Season the lamb shanks with salt and black pepper and serve with the bone pointing up. Pour the sauce over the lamb shanks and garnish with the thyme leaves and sprigs.

In defense of those who have overcooked lobster in the past, it's easy to do using conventional cooking methods. Using sous vide, however, it's reasonably simple to create the silky, moist, soft lobster of your dreams (okay, that was a bit dramatic, but you may not have ever tasted lobster quite like this). There are many conflicting opinions out there on what temperature is ideal to cook lobster sous vide. After plenty of trial and error, I believe that 133°F/56°C for 15 minutes makes the tails just-cooked, which is the way they should be (in my opinion). By cooking it for longer at a lower temperature than you would if you boiled it, you're able to get a less rubbery texture, and definitely no dryness.

BUTTER-POACHED LOBSTER TAILS

🌡 133°F/56°C　|　⏱ 15 MINUTES　|　🍴 SERVES 4

INGREDIENTS

4 lobster tails, speared with a knife or skewer (see page 25)

8 tablespoons/113 g unsalted butter, divided

2 garlic cloves, crushed

Sea salt to taste

DIRECTIONS

Preheat a sous vide water bath to 133°F/56°C.

Bring a large pot of water to a boil. Submerge the speared lobster tails in the boiling water and remove the pot from the heat immediately. Leave the lobster tails in the water for 2 minutes, then remove and immediately submerge in an ice bath. With scissors, carefully remove the lobster shells.

Combine 4 tablespoons/56 g of the butter, garlic, and salt in a skillet over medium heat. Heat until the butter has browned, approximately 1 to 2 minutes, then transfer to a small bowl to stop the cooking.

Seal the peeled lobster tails in vacuum-seal bags, one per bag, with the butter-garlic mixture. Cook in the preheated water bath for 15 minutes.

A few minutes before the sous vide cooking is complete, heat a skillet over medium heat and brown the remaining 4 tablespoons/56 g of butter. When the lobster has finished cooking sous vide, cut open the bag and pour the liquid contents from it into the skillet. Stir to combine, and then transfer the sauce to a sauceboat, small bowl, or any container that will allow you to pour the sauce reasonably accurately over the tail.

Carefully transfer the tails to serving plates, and pour the butter sauce over the top.

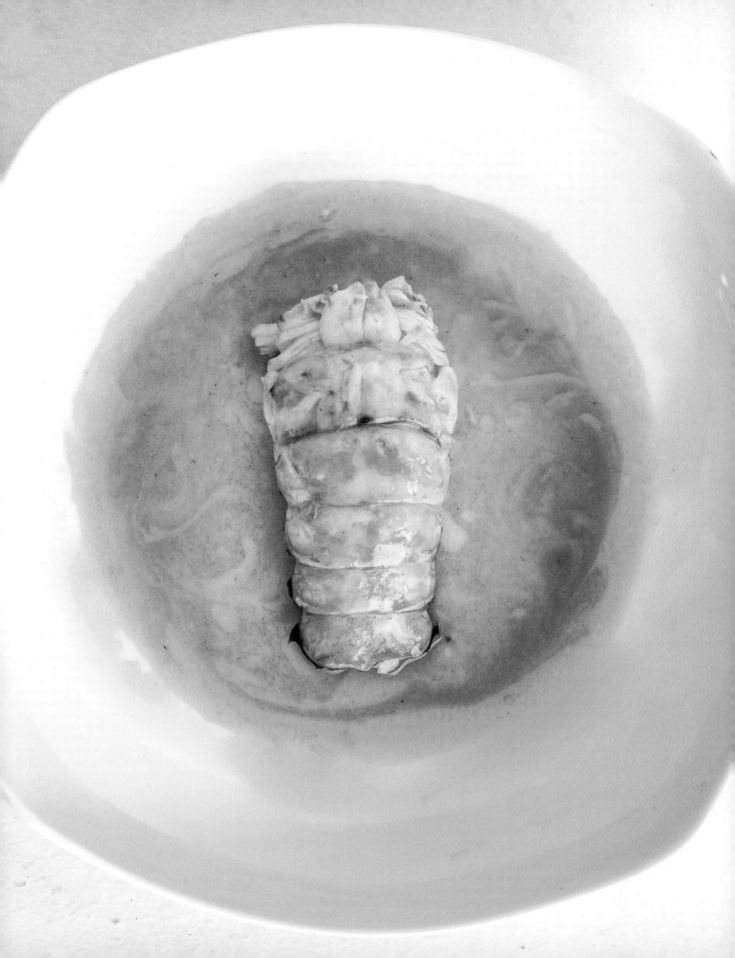

Most of the time, keeping a recipe simple is the best way to enjoy the subtle taste of fresh fish. This recipe is built to let the fish shine, with accents of lemon, olive oil, and capers. Cooking fish sous vide is a fantastic way to ensure that your fillet is perfectly cooked, and not dry in the slightest. However, sous vide cooked fish is very fragile, so you'll need to be very careful when you remove it from the bag to ensure it doesn't break.

Additionally, when cooking delicate foods such as white fish, it's worth bearing in mind that any substantial seasonings that you place in the bag, like lemon slices or thick-stemmed herbs, will leave a mark on the surface of the fish—so you might want to serve the fish with the seasoning still on top. That's what I've done here with the lemon slices.

LEMON-INFUSED WHITE FISH

🌡 131°F/55°C | ⏱ 30 MINUTES (SEE NOTE) | 🍴 SERVES 4

INGREDIENTS

4 slices lemon

4 (6- to 7-ounce/170- to 200-g) skinless white fish fillets, such as cod or halibut

1 cup/240 ml olive oil

4 teaspoons/11½ g drained capers

Sea salt and black pepper

PEA PURÉE

2 cups/320 g frozen peas

2 tablespoons/28 g unsalted butter

2 garlic cloves

¼ cup/60 ml cream

Sea salt and black pepper

Note: The timing in this recipe is based on a fillet that's 1 to 1½ inches thick. If you have a much thinner piece, reduce the cooking time to 20 minutes.

DIRECTIONS

Preheat a sous vide water bath to 131°F/55°C.

Place a lemon slice on each fish fillet and place each in individual resealable plastic bags. Add a few tablespoons of the olive oil to each bag and seal the bags using the displacement method (page 14). Clip the bags to the side of the pot and cook in the preheated water bath for 30 minutes.

While the fish cooks, make the purée. Cook the peas according to the package instructions, then drain. Heat the butter in a frying pan over medium heat, add the garlic, and fry until it has browned. Add the drained peas, cream, and salt and pepper to taste and stir to combine. Transfer to a food processor and blitz until it's puréed to your desired consistency.

When the fish is done, divide the pea purée among 4 plates. Remove the fish from the bag, discarding any cooking liquid, and place the fish on top of the purée (keep the lemon on top of the fish). Scatter the capers over the fish and drizzle 1 tablespoon olive oil over the top. Season with salt and black pepper to taste.

Shrimp, along with chicken and calamari, is notoriously easy to overcook. In fact, it's even easy to overcook shrimp when using sous vide! I've read numerous recipes for sous vide shrimp that use a higher temperature than I've mentioned here, and when I followed them, the shrimp became mushy. That led me to conduct an elaborate shrimp-testing experiment using a variety of temperatures. I found that when cooked at 135°F/57°C for 15 minutes, small-to medium-size shrimp come out perfect.

This Spanish classic is a fantastic way to show off your sous vide shrimp. There are many variations of this popular appetizer, but the key ingredients generally remain the same: shrimp, garlic, and olive oil. Cook them to perfection using sous vide and then serve them in chile and garlic oil with some crusty bread to mop up all the juicy goodness.

SHRIMP GAMBAS

🌡 135°F/57°C | ⏱ 15 MINUTES | 🍴 SERVES 4

INGREDIENTS

1 pound/450 g medium-size shrimp, shelled and deveined

½ cup/120 ml olive oil

10 garlic cloves, sliced

1 teaspoon/2 g paprika

½ to 1 teaspoon/1 to 2 g red pepper flakes (depending on how much spice you like)

2 teaspoons/10 ml lemon juice, plus lemon wedges to serve

3 tablespoons/18¾ g chopped fresh parsley

Sea salt and black pepper

1 loaf of rye bread, sliced

DIRECTIONS

Preheat a sous vide water bath to 135°F/57°C.

Lay the shrimp flat in vacuum-seal bags, seal, and cook in the preheated water bath for 15 minutes.

When the shrimp has finished cooking sous vide, cut open the bag and pour any liquid into a small pot, then set it on a burner over medium heat. Once the liquid warms, add the olive oil to the pot and let it warm for about a minute. Fry the garlic slices in the oil for a couple of minutes until they begin to turn golden, then take the pot off the heat and stir in the paprika, red pepper flakes, lemon juice, parsley, and salt and pepper to taste.

Leave the pot off the heat while you toast the slices of rye bread.

When the bread is toasted, add the shrimp to the chile and garlic oil, stir well to coat the shrimp, and serve in dishes alongside the toasted rye bread.

I know many people who get put off of recipes when they see that they have to make a roux, so I wanted to create a macaroni recipe that did away with that element. Yet it wasn't as simple as I thought it would be to get the macaroni doneness right and the thickness of the sauce the way I wanted it. In the end, I found the happy medium that gave me the creamy mac 'n' cheese that I was after. I tend to eat this mac 'n' cheese straight out of the bowl when it's finished cooking sous vide, but if you prefer a crispy crust on top of yours, follow the optional crust instructions at the end of this recipe.

EASY 'N' CREAMY MAC 'N' CHEESE

♨ 170°F/77°C | ⏲ 1 HOUR | ✕ SERVES 4 TO 6

INGREDIENTS

10 ounces/285 g elbow macaroni

2 cups/475 ml whole milk

2 cups/475 ml evaporated milk

2 tablespoons/28 g unsalted butter, melted

2 heaping teaspoons mustard powder

2 teaspoons/7 g garlic salt

1 teaspoon/5 g black pepper

1 cup/113 g grated Cheddar cheese

1 cup/113 g grated red Cheddar cheese

1 cup/113 g grated Gruyère cheese

OPTIONAL BAKED TOPPING

3 tablespoons unsalted butter

1 cup panko bread crumbs

DIRECTIONS

Preheat a sous vide water bath to 170°F/77°C.

Bring a pot of water to a boil for the macaroni. Boil the pasta for 5 minutes, then drain and set aside.

In a large bowl, combine the milk and evaporated milk, then stir in the melted butter. Add the mustard powder, garlic salt, pepper, and cheeses. Finally, add the cooked macaroni and stir to combine.

Divide the mixture among 4 resealable plastic bags. Submerge the bags into the preheated water bath using the displacement method (see page 14). Clip the bags to the edge of the preheated water bath, and cook for 1 hour.

When the hour is up, pour the contents of the bags into a large dish (use a baking dish if it will be going in the oven) and stir to combine. From here, you can season to taste with salt and pepper and serve immediately, or you can top it with a variety of ingredients.

For an optional baked topping, preheat the oven to 350°F/177°C. Melt the butter in a sauté pan over medium heat. Add the bread crumbs and toss in the pan until combined, about 1 minute. Sprinkle the bread crumbs over the mac 'n' cheese and bake for 30 minutes, or until crispy.

With pumpkin and the earthy flavors of brown butter, this pasta is a fantastic savory dish for fall. Make sure you buy a pumpkin variety that's suitable for eating—skip the carving pumpkins. Instead, try one of the many flavorful varieties of squash such as delicata, kabocha, or red kuri.

PUMPKIN, SAGE, AND BROWN BUTTER PASTA

✺ 180°F/82°C | ⏱ 1 HOUR 30 MINUTES | 🍴 SERVES 4

INGREDIENTS

2 pounds/900 g pumpkin or squash, peeled and chopped into 1-inch pieces

Pasta of your choice (fettuccini works well)

4 tablespoons/56 g unsalted butter

3 garlic cloves, finely diced

10 sage leaves

1 tablespoon/5 ml freshly squeezed lemon juice

¼ cup/25 g grated Parmesan

Salt and black pepper

DIRECTIONS

Preheat a sous vide water bath to 180°F/82°C.

Vacuum seal the pumpkin or squash chunks in one or more bags and cook in the preheated water bath for 1 hour 30 minutes. When the time is up, check to make sure the pumpkin is cooked by squeezing it between your fingers through the bag (it should squash without too much pressure). Cook for longer if needed. Set the bag aside on the counter.

Cook the pasta according to the package directions.

While the pasta cooks, melt the butter in a medium-size pot over medium heat and add the garlic. Cook until the butter turns golden brown, and then add the sage leaves. Add the cooked pumpkin or squash and stir to coat well with the butter. Squeeze in the lemon juice and remove the pan from the heat.

Drain the pasta once it's done, reserving ¼ cup/60 ml of the cooking water. Add the cheese to the pumpkin sauce and stir in the pasta. Stir in 1 tablespoon of cooking water at a time, until it reaches a moistness level you're happy with (you may not want to use it all). Add salt and pepper to taste. Serve immediately.

It's tough to beat a juicy burger topped with melted cheese, enjoyed in the backyard on a sunny day. Whether you prefer your burger cooked through or still pink in the middle, you can nail it every time with sous vide. The temperature listed in this recipe is for a medium rare burger, but see the temperature guide below if you like your burger done differently. A word on thickness: yes, at 1½ to 2 inches, these are some fat burgers. But to really make the most of cooking them sous vide and to ensure that you minimize the risk of overcooking when you grill them, it's best to try them on the larger side first. As with any meat, the amount of time a burger needs in the sous vide water bath depends on its thickness. So a thicker burger will need longer, and a thinner burger won't need as much time if you decide to adjust your patties.

THE NEW BACKYARD BURGER

🌡 130°F/54°C | 🕐 1½ HOURS | 🍴 SERVES 4

INGREDIENTS

1½ pounds/680 g good-quality ground beef

1 egg

2 tablespoons bread crumbs

1 teaspoon/6 g yellow mustard

Sea salt and freshly ground black pepper to taste

RECOMMENDED FOR ASSEMBLY:

4 slices American cheese or the cheese of your choice

4 burger buns, halved and toasted

Your favorite burger toppings

DIRECTIONS

Preheat a sous vide water bath to 130°F/51°C. This will yield a perfect medium rare burger after finishing, but you can adjust the temperature as you'd like:

DONENESS LEVEL	TEMPERATURE
RARE	120°F (49°C)
MEDIUM RARE	130°F (54°C)
MEDIUM	135°F (57°C)
MEDIUM WELL	145°F (63°C)
WELL DONE	156°F (69°C+)

In a large mixing bowl, combine the beef, egg, bread crumbs, yellow mustard, and salt and pepper to taste. Mix by hand until the ingredients are well combined, then divide into 4 equal portions and form into patties. Compact the patties just a bit, enough so that they stick together well and no ground beef is falling off the patty.

Seal the patties individually in resealable plastic bags using the displacement method (see page 14), clip the bag to the side of the preheated water bath, and cook for 1½ hours.

Now it's time to fire up the grill. Grilling a sous vide burger is unlike cooking a burger from raw because the burger is already cooked to optimal doneness. Instead of *cooking* it on the grill, you're just using the fiery heat to get a good char on the outside. This means you only need to cook it for 1 minute on each side on a very hot grill.

If you're using a gas grill, turn it on high and close the lid for 5 to 10 minutes. If you're using a coal grill, light the coals and let them burn for 5 to 10 minutes. Place the burgers on the grill for 1 minute on each side, placing the cheese on the top for the second minute.

Note: If you want to use a blowtorch for some extra char, grill for 30 seconds, then flip. Torch the top of the patty that was just on the grill, while the other side cooks on the grill surface, then flip and repeat. For these last 30 seconds, place a slice of cheese on the burger and use this time to allow it to melt a little. Shaving 30 seconds off of the 2-minute cooking time will help compensate for the extra heat you added with the blowtorch.

Serve your perfect patties in buns with your favorite toppings.

With sous vide you can actually cook pork without any sauce for 24 hours and end up with moist meat ready for any sauce. However, in this recipe we'll cook the pork together with the sauce to really infuse the meat with those barbecue flavors. To that end, I have adapted my favorite barbecue sauce (page 73) for this recipe because we want to cook the pork with some of it in the bag. When cooking sous vide for long periods of time, you don't want a lot of salt in the bag, or the meat will begin to brine. For that reason, we will reduce the amount of ketchup and not add the ketchup and salt until the very end, after sous vide.

PULLED PORK SLIDERS WITH APPLE SLAW

🌡 158°F/70°C | ⏲ 24 HOURS | 🍴 SERVES 4 (MAKES 12 SLIDERS)

INGREDIENTS

LOW-SALT BARBECUE SAUCE

1 tablespoon/14 g unsalted butter

1 tablespoon/15 ml vegetable oil

2 tablespoons/8 g finely diced onion

6 garlic cloves, finely diced

¼ cup/53 g firmly packed brown sugar

3 tablespoons/45 ml apple cider vinegar

2 tablespoons/30 ml water

¾ cup/185 g tomato paste

1 tablespoon/15 g paprika

1 tablespoon/15 ml Worcestershire sauce

1 teaspoon 5 g black pepper

1 cup/240 g ketchup

Salt to taste

PORK

1 pork shoulder (about 1¼ pounds/600 g)

12 slider buns

½ cup/25 g cilantro leaves

APPLE SLAW

4 green apples, peeled and julienned

1 cup/64 g julienned scallion, stalks and ends removed

1 carrot, peeled and julienned

1 cup/100 g julienned cabbage

3 long red chiles, seeded and julienned

⅓ cup/75 g mayonnaise

1 tablespoon/15 ml white vinegar

1 tablespoon/30 ml honey

Salt and black pepper to taste

DIRECTIONS

Preheat a sous vide water bath to 158°F/70°C.

To make the barbecue sauce, heat a saucepan over medium heat. Add the butter and let it melt. Add the vegetable oil and fry the onion and garlic for a few minutes, until the onion softens and the butter browns. Add the brown sugar and vinegar and decrease the heat to low. Cook for 15 minutes, adding the water after about 5 minutes, or when the sauce gets very sticky. After 15 minutes, add the tomato paste, paprika, Worcestershire sauce, and pepper. Scrape any garlic and onion bits off the bottom with a spatula so they combine with the sauce. Bring the sauce to a boil over high heat, then immediately decrease the heat and gently simmer for about 20 minutes. Remove from the heat. Transfer about ¼ cup/60 ml of the sauce to a separate container. Stir the ketchup and salt to taste into the remaining barbecue sauce, then transfer to a container, cover, and store in the fridge.

To make the pork, brush the reserved ¼ cup/60 ml of ketchup-less sauce all over the pork shoulder. Seal it in a vacuum-seal bag, or cut it in half and seal in 2 bags depending on the size of your bags. Cook in the preheated water bath for 24 hours.

The next day, just before the pork has finished cooking, make the apple slaw. Combine all of the slaw ingredients in a large bowl and stir well to blend. To keep it crunchy, I recommend doing this just before the pork finishes cooking or just after you shred the pork. This slaw is best right after it's made!

Once the pork has finished cooking, shred the meat with 2 forks and combine it with the barbecue sauce. Divide the pork evenly among the slider buns and top it with the slaw and cilantro leaves.

Fall-off-the-bone ribs are what most people are after, whether they're eating out or cooking ribs at home. Yet the long, semi-active cooking time can be a major inconvenience. And on the other side, ribs in a slow cooker can get too soft. My solution, of course, is to cook them sous vide. I cover them in a dry rub without salt so that I can impart flavor into the meat during cooking while ensuring that the rub does not cause the meat to brine. Finally, I finish my ribs with barbecue sauce just before a quick hit of heat from the grill or broiler to finish.

BABY BACK RIBS WITH BOURBON BARBECUE SAUCE

🌡 158°F/70°C | ⏱ 24 HOURS | 🍴 SERVES 4

INGREDIENTS

¼ cup/60 ml olive oil

2 full racks baby back pork ribs, trimmed

SALT-FREE BARBECUE RUB

2 tablespoons smoked paprika

2 tablespoons/53 g firmly packed brown sugar

1 tablespoon/15 g black pepper

1 tablespoon/15 g chili powder

1 tablespoon/15 g onion powder

1 tablespoon/15 g garlic powder

BOURBON BARBECUE SAUCE

1 tablespoon/14 g unsalted butter

1 tablespoon/15 ml vegetable oil

2 tablespoons/16 g finely diced onion

6 garlic cloves, minced

3 tablespoons/79 g firmly packed brown sugar

5 tablespoons/75 ml apple cider vinegar

2 tablespoons/30 ml water

½ cup/120 ml bourbon whiskey

1 tablespoon/15 g paprika

1 to 2 teaspoons/5 to 10 g chili powder, to taste

1¼ cups/300 g ketchup

¾ cup/130 g tomato paste

1 tablespoon Worcestershire sauce

1 teaspoon/5 g black pepper

1 teaspoon/5 g salt

DIRECTIONS

Preheat a sous vide water bath to 158°F/70°C.

Rub the olive oil onto the pork ribs.

To make the rub, combine all of the ingredients in a small bowl. Massage the rub all over the ribs. Seal each rack of ribs in individual vacuum-seal bags and cook in the preheated water bath for 24 hours.

To make the barbecue sauce, place a saucepan over medium heat. Add the butter and let it melt, then add the vegetable oil and fry the onion and garlic for a few minutes, until the onion softens and the butter browns. Add the brown sugar and vinegar and decrease the heat to low. Cook for 15 minutes, adding the water after about 5 minutes, or when the sauce gets very sticky. Stir every few minutes and scrape up any bits from the bottom of the pot. After 15 minutes of caramelizing, add the whiskey and turn the heat up to high. Boil for a few minutes to burn off some of the alcohol, then add the paprika, chili powder, ketchup, tomato paste, Worcestershire sauce, pepper, and salt, scraping any garlic and onion off the bottom with a spatula. Bring to a boil over high heat, then decrease the heat and simmer for 20 minutes, or until the flavors develop and the sauce thickens. Transfer to a storage container and refrigerate until the next day.

The next day, about 10 minutes before the ribs have finished cooking sous vide, prepare to finish them by taking the sauce out of the fridge and preheating your broiler or grill to high. When the time is up, take the ribs out of the bag and baste with the sauce. You can either grill or broil them, and complement both of those methods with a blowtorch (optional).

To broil the ribs, place the basted ribs on a baking tray covered in foil. Place them under the broiler for about 2 minutes, or until they start to brown. Don't leave them until really brown or you'll overcook the meat. If you want to char the surface further, use a blowtorch (see pages 33 to 35).

To grill the ribs, place the basted ribs directly on well-oiled grill grates, with the top facing down. Do not cover, and grill for only 1 minute, or until just browned. Just as with broiling, you can let them start to get color but you can't really char them without a risk of overcooking. If you want to develop additional browning, use a blowtorch (see pages 33 to 35).

When it comes to beef ribs, tenderness is key. Just as with the pork ribs, cooking sous vide will get you tender ribs every time without requiring nearly as much work as traditional low and slow cooking. Since the beef ribs are a bit tougher to start, you'll cook the ribs sous vide for double the time of pork: 48 hours. As far as adding some smoke flavor, I've found that an easy home smoking method using wood chips or tea leaves can add a good amount of smoke flavor in a short amount of time. Get ready for some insanely tender, seriously delicious beef ribs! If you'd like to serve it with barbecue sauce, there are a couple recipes to choose from on pages 71 and 73. You can even add the cooking liquid from the ribs to one of those sauces! Just incorporate it after the rest of the sauce has been prepared and cook the sauce back down a bit to remove the excess water.

SMOKED BEEF RIBS

🌡 158°F/70°C | ⏱ 48 HOURS | 🍴 SERVES 4

Note: This time is for falling-apart doneness; if you prefer your ribs meatier, you can reduce the cooking time to 36 hours. You can check on it during cooking to assess its tenderness by pressing on the meat with your fingers through the bag to see how much it gives/falls apart. If you are not able to ascertain the texture by pressing, you can always cut open the bag and test, then seal it up again (in a new bag, if necessary) before submerging it back into the water.

INGREDIENTS

¼ cup/60 ml olive oil

1 rack beef spare ribs, trimmed

1 tablespoon/15 g smoked salt (you can use regular salt if you'd like, but the smoked salt will help boost the smoky flavor)

SALT-FREE RUB

2 tablespoons smoked paprika

2 tablespoons/53 g firmly packed brown sugar

1 tablespoon/15 g black pepper

1 tablespoon/15 g chili powder

1 tablespoon/15 g mustard powder

1 tablespoon/15 g onion powder

1 tablespoon/15 g garlic powder

Note: I have suggested finishing these ribs with a DIY smoker and a torch, but they are also fantastic when finished on the grill or in a pan (with optional but recommended torch for both methods).

DIRECTIONS

Preheat a sous vide water bath to 158°F/70°C.

Rub the olive oil onto all sides of the beef ribs.

To make the rub, combine all of the ingredients in a small bowl. Massage the rub all over the ribs. Seal the ribs in 1 or 2 vacuum-seal bags, depending on the size of each, and cook in the preheated water bath for 48 hours.

When the ribs have finished cooking sous vide, take them out of the vacuum-seal bags and place on a large chopping board; do this carefully because they will be very tender and you don't want the bones to separate from the meat. Reserve the cooking liquid if you'd like to incorporate it into a barbecue sauce.

At this point, cover the ribs in the smoked salt and prepare the DIY smoker, if using. If you'd prefer to grill them, see my guide to grilling on pages 35 and 74. For pan searing them, see my guide to pan searing on pages 31 to 33.

DIY SMOKER

This DIY smoker uses equipment that you probably already have around the house. You can choose to smoke with either wood chips or a tea mixture, depending on which one you can source more easily.

WHAT YOU'LL NEED:

A wok or large pot

Foil

A grill tray or microwave rack

Additional foil or a pot (to enclose the smoke)

Woodchips or tea mixture

WOOD CHIPS

A few handfuls of wood chips for smoking (mesquite, apple, cherry, oak and hickory work well).

Note: Soak a few handfuls of chips in water for 30 minutes before use. Then drain and put 1 or 2 handfuls of chips into your DIY smoker.

TEA MIXTURE

2 tablespoons/30 g tea leaves (you can use black, green, jasmine, Earl Gray, or even lapsang souchong, which has a smoky flavor of its own)

2 tablespoons/24 g rice

2 tablespoons/23 g firmly packed brown sugar

Note: To make the tea mixture, simply combine all of the ingredients in a small bowl.

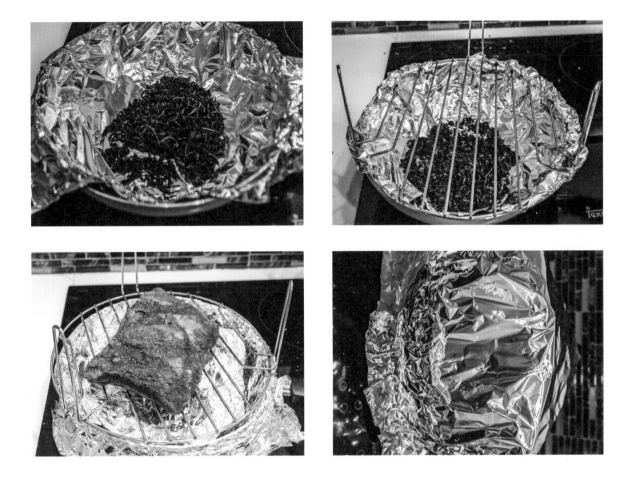

DIRECTIONS

To set up the smoker, line a wok with foil and put either the pre-soaked woodchips or tea mixture onto the foil. Place the wok over high heat if using woodchips, or medium heat if using the tea mixture. Allow the contents to heat until they smoke, about 10 minutes. Once smoking, cover the wok with a microwave stand or grill tray and carefully put the rack of ribs on top. If you can't fit a whole rack at once, work in batches rather than stacking the ribs. To contain the smoke, cover everything with a pot lid, large pot, or with foil.

Smoke the ribs for 20 minutes, then carefully remove so as not to separate the meat from the bone. If you have ribs left to smoke, repeat the process (using fresh tea mixture or wood chips). When you've finished smoking, I recommend removing the lid of your DIY smoker and finishing the ribs with a good blast with a torch for extra char (see my guide to torching on page 33 to 35).

Tough cuts of meat like brisket really benefit from slow cooking. By using sous vide for your slow cooking, you can get tender, juicy brisket with a surprise inside—even after all that time, it's still pink in the middle. Although the cooking time may seem long, there's actually very little work involved in this recipe. Like the beef ribs on page 75, I've used a salt-free dry rub to ensure the meat doesn't brine during the long cooking time, so all you need to do is add the salt at the end to complete the seasoning. Grilling the brisket just before serving or experimenting with the smoking method on pages 78 and 79 will give you the most additional flavor, but this beef is equally delicious if you choose to sear it after sous vide in a hot frying pan.

72-HOUR BEEF BRISKET

🌡 135°F/57°C | ⏱ 72 HOURS | 🍴 SERVES 4 TO 6

INGREDIENTS

SALT-FREE RUB

2 tablespoons smoked paprika

2 tablespoons/23 g firmly packed brown sugar

1 tablespoon/15 g black pepper

1 tablespoon/15 g chili powder

1 tablespoon/15 g mustard powder

1 tablespoon/15 g onion powder

1 tablespoon/15 g garlic powder

BRISKET

About 2 pounds/900 g beef brisket

¼ cup/60 ml olive oil

1 tablespoon/20 g salt or smoked salt (use a good-quality smoked salt if you can find it

Note: This time is for falling-apart doneness; if you prefer your brisket meatier, you can reduce the cooking time to 60 hours. You can check on it during cooking to assess its tenderness by pressing on the meat with your fingers through the bag to see how much it gives/falls apart. If you are not able to ascertain the texture by pressing, you can always cut open the bag and test, then seal it up again (in a new bag, if necessary) before submerging it back into the water.

DIRECTIONS

Preheat a sous vide water bath to 135°F/57°C.

To make the rub, combine all the ingredients in a small bowl.

To make the brisket, coat the meat with a thin layer of olive oil, and then coat well with the dry rub. Seal the brisket in a large vacuum-seal bag, or cut in half and seal in 2 bags. Cook in the preheated water bath for 72 hours.

When the brisket has finished cooking sous vide, rub it with the salt. To finish, you have a few options:

- To grill the brisket, preheat your grill for 5 to 10 minutes until very hot, and place the brisket on well-oiled grates for about 2 minutes on all 4 sides. You want to get some char on the outside but not dry out the meat.

- To smoke the brisket, you can give it 20 minutes in my DIY smoker. Follow the instructions on pages 78 and 79.

- To fry the brisket, heat a frying pan until smoking hot. Add 2 tablespoons vegetable oil and 2 tablespoons butter to the pan. Sear the brisket well on all 4 sides, 2 to 2½ minutes each side, or until you get a good sear. As brisket is quite thick (compared to a steak, for example), so you can cook it for slightly longer without the risk of overcooking the meat. Make sure you get a good crust, but remember that steam coming off is moisture leaving your precious brisket, so don't leave it in there for too long! (Additionally, you don't want the butter to burn and smoke.)

Slice the brisket thin with a sharp knife and serve immediately. This goes fantastically with my Bourbon Barbecue Sauce (page 73).

This beef "Wellington" takes the best parts of the iconic dish and reimagines them—taking full advantage of sous vide. This means instead of a log of beef, my Wellington is built on individual fillet steaks. In the place of pâté, I've got a nice creamy chunk of foie gras. And since we don't want to overcook our beautifully tender sous vide steak, the pastry is cooked separately and popped on top like a crisp, buttery hat.

DECONSTRUCTED BEEF "WELLINGTON"

🌡 129°F/54°C | ⏱ 2 HOURS | 🍴 SERVES 4

INGREDIENTS

4 fillet steaks (8 ounces/ 230 g each)

8 ounces/230 g puff pastry, thawed

2 egg yolks beaten with 2 tablespoons/30 ml whole milk

4 slices foie gras, lightly scored on each side

Salt and black pepper

MUSHROOM RED WINE SAUCE

4 tablespoons/56 g unsalted butter

2 cups/140 g finely diced baby portobello or white button mushrooms

2 teaspoons/2 g fresh thyme leaves

2 teaspoons/2 g chopped fresh rosemary

1 cup/240 ml dry red wine

Salt and black pepper

DIRECTIONS

Preheat a sous vide water bath to 129°F/54°C.

Seal the steaks in vacuum-seal bags and cook in the preheated water bath for 2 hours.

With half an hour left on the steaks, preheat your oven to 450°F/232°C. When the oven is hot, cut the pastry into 4 rounds (one per steak) about the same size as the steaks and paint with the beaten egg. Transfer to a parchment-lined baking sheet and bake until golden brown, about 8 minutes. When the pastry is cooked and golden, remove the baking tray from the oven and set aside.

When the steaks have around 15 to 20 minutes left of sous vide cooking, begin making the sauce (don't worry if you go over time; the steaks will be fine in the sous vide water bath for a little longer). Heat a small pot over medium-low heat and add the butter. Toss in the mushrooms, thyme, and rosemary and cook for about 10 minutes. Turn the heat up to high and add the red wine. Stirring occasionally, continue to cook for 5 to 10 minutes, or until you have about 6 tablespoons of liquid left, then remove from the heat.

While the wine is reducing, heat a dry skillet over high heat until it's smoking. Generously season the foie gras with salt and pepper. Sear for 20 to 30 seconds on each side, or until you get some good color, then set aside on a chopping board and cover with foil.

Return the skillet to high heat, keeping any foie gras fat in the pan. Take the steaks out of the vacuum-seal bags (reserving any liquid from the bags), pat them dry, and generously season with salt and pepper. Sear the steaks in the foie gras fat for 1 to 1½ minutes on each side, or until you get some good color, then immediately remove them from the skillet and set them aside on the cutting board and cover with foil.

Lay out 4 plates to make individual servings. Place a steak on each plate and spoon the sauce over the top. Place the foie gras on the steak, and then top each with 1 pastry round.

The Brits love a good pork belly, be it in a classic roast or in this slightly more refined dish. After 24 hours of sous vide cooking, the fatty pork belly is juicy and tender, but doesn't fall apart like pulled pork unless you really try to shred it. Any tough elements have been well and truly broken down, but the pork holds its shape enough for you to slice it with a sharp knife. For this recipe, you can brine the pork before cooking sous vide, which will help it retain some extra moisture, although it will also add an extra 24 hours onto the recipe time!

24-HOUR PORK BELLY WITH POTATO PURÉE AND CARAMELIZED APPLE

♨* 158°F/70°C | ⏲ 24 HOURS | ✗ SERVES 6

INGREDIENTS

BRINE

1 quart/1 L water

⅓ cup/82 g kosher salt

¼ cup/50 g sugar

PORK BELLY

2 pounds/900 g pork belly

¼ cup/60 ml vegetable oil

POTATO PURÉE

3 medium potatoes, peeled and quartered (Yukon Gold potatoes work well here)

Salt to taste

3 tablespoons/45 ml milk

3 tablespoons/42 g unsalted butter

CARAMELIZED APPLES

2 tablespoons/28 g unsalted butter

2 teaspoons/10 ml freshly squeezed lemon juice

2 teaspoons/30 ml honey or sugar

1 green apple, cored and sliced into ¼-inch/5-mm slices

DIRECTIONS

If you're brining the pork belly, whisk the brine ingredients together in a large bowl and submerge the pork. Cover and refrigerate for 24 hours, flipping the pork around in the brine halfway through.

The next day, preheat a sous vide water bath to 158°F/70°C.

Seal the pork in a vacuum-seal bag, or if you don't have a large enough bag, cut the pork in half and use 2 bags. Cook in the preheated water bath for 24 hours.

When the pork has around 45 minutes of sous vide cooking time left, start the water for the potatoes. Boil the potato quarters in salted water until fork-tender, 5 to 10 minutes depending on their size. Drain the potatoes and transfer to a blender along with the milk, butter, and salt to taste. Blend until smooth. Cover and set aside while you finish the other components.

To make the apples, melt the butter in a frying pan over medium-low heat. Add the lemon juice and stir in the honey until it has completely dissolved. Arrange the apple slices in the pan and cook until caramelized, around 15 minutes, moving them in the pan occasionally and flipping halfway through.

When the pork has finished cooking sous vide, remove it from the bag (or bags) and trim it with a sharp knife into 2½-inch/6 mm cubes. Heat a frying pan over high heat, then add the vegetable oil. Fry the pork belly skin-side down a few at a time without crowding the pan, until the top is browned, 3 to 4 minutes. Repeat until all of the pieces are browned.

Spoon the potato purée onto each plate and arrange the pork and apple slices on top.

Seared with a flavor-packed rub and perfectly medium rare in the middle, this rack of lamb is a showstopper when you're feeding a crowd. They'll never know it requires hardly any work! Cooking the lamb sous vide ensures the meat is perfectly cooked all the way through, with no overcooked bits on the edges, which is what often happens when you cook lamb in the oven. And with a cooking time of 2½ hours, it'll get some good tenderizing too.

Since one rack of lamb has 7 or 8 ribs, two racks gives you between 14 and 16 ribs—that's enough for 7 or 8 people to have 2 ribs each. You may want to adjust your serving size depending on the racks you buy and how many ribs they have.

ROSEMARY AND GARLIC RACK OF LAMB

🌡 130°F/54°C | ⏱ 2½ HOURS | 🍴 SERVES 8

INGREDIENTS

2 tablespoons/30 g mustard powder

2 tablespoons/23 g firmly packed brown sugar

2 tablespoons/30 g paprika

2 racks of lamb, French trimmed

8 garlic cloves

4 sprigs fresh rosemary, leaves only

2 teaspoons/15 g salt

2 teaspoons/15 g black pepper

4 tablespoons/56 g unsalted butter, divided

½ wedge preserved lemon (see page 277; optional)

DIRECTIONS

Preheat a sous vide water bath to 130°F/54°C.

Combine the mustard powder, brown sugar, and paprika in a small bowl, then coat the lamb well with the mixture. Seal the racks in individual vacuum-seal bags and cook in the preheated water bath for 2½ hours.

Just before the lamb has finished cooking, pound the garlic cloves, rosemary leaves, preserved lemon (if using) salt, and pepper with a mortar and pestle until it forms a rub with a paste-like consistency. Once the lamb has finished cooking, remove it from the bags, discarding any liquid, and rub it with the garlic-rosemary mixture. Set aside.

Heat a large frying pan until it's smoking hot. Add 2 tablespoons of the butter to the pan and sear one of the lamb racks on all exposed sides until brown, 1 to 1½ minutes on each side, or until browned on all sides. Pour the burnt butter out into a small bowl and reserve. Give the frying pan a quick wipe with paper towels and repeat the process with the remaining 2 tablespoons butter and the second rack.

To serve, slice the lamb into cutlets and drizzle some of the burnt butter over the top.

This deliciously meaty, umami-rich dish is perfect for those who love the unique flavor of lamb. After cooking at 140°F/60°C for 24 hours, the lamb is extremely tender yet also still has a bit of pink in the middle. This feat is almost impossible to achieve with traditional slow-cooking methods. To complement the rich, meaty base, I've included plenty of fresh herbs.

SHREDDED LAMB AND MUSHROOM RAGU

🌡 140°F/60°C | ⏲ 24 HOURS | 🍴 SERVES 4

INGREDIENTS

LAMB

1 pound/450 g lamb shoulder

1 onion, finely chopped

1 carrot, finely chopped

1 stalk celery, finely chopped

2 tablespoons/33 g tomato paste

SAUCE

2 tablespoons/28 g unsalted butter

2 cups/156 g porcini mushrooms (or similar), sliced

4 garlic cloves, minced

½ cup/120 ml red wine

1 can (28 ounces/800 g) chopped tomatoes

1 cup/240 ml beef stock

2 bay leaves

2 tablespoons/12½ g chopped fresh basil

2 tablespoons/12½ g chopped fresh parsley

FOR SERVING

1 pound/450 g pasta of your choice

¼ to ½ cup/25 to 50 g grated Parmesan

Salt and black pepper

DIRECTIONS

Preheat a sous vide water bath to 140°F/60°C.

To make the lamb, place the lamb in a large vacuum-seal bag with the onion, carrot, celery, and tomato paste and seal. Cook in the preheated water bath for 24 hours.

To make the sauce, about 30 minutes before the lamb is done, heat a saucepan over medium heat and melt the butter. Fry the mushrooms for 10 minutes, then add the garlic and fry for a few more minutes. Turn the heat up to medium-high and pour in the red wine. Stir until most of the wine has been absorbed, 5 to 10 minutes.

As the wine cooks into the mushrooms, remove the lamb from the bag and pour the rest of the contents from the bag into the pot. Return the lamb to the bag and clip it to the edge of the water bath to keep it warm.

Add the chopped tomatoes, beef stock, bay leaves, basil, and 1 tablespoon of the chopped parsley to the pot. Bring the mixture to a boil and then decrease the heat to medium-low. Simmer for 20 minutes to allow the flavors to infuse and some of the liquid to evaporate.

To serve, cook the pasta according to the package instructions, and then drain. This should happen close to the time the lamb and sauce are ready. If not, you can toss the pasta with a bit of oil to keep it from sticking together.

After 20 minutes, take the lamb out of the water bath. Shred it into bite-size pieces and stir it into the sauce. Remove and discard the bay leaves. Transfer the sauce to a large bowl and stir in the cooked pasta. Serve topped with Parmesan, the remaining 1 tablespoon chopped parsley, and salt and pepper to taste.

As with a lot of sous vide foods, the chicken in this recipe is not ready to serve right after it comes out of the bag. You cook it sous vide first, and then batter it and deep-fry it. Why do two steps instead of one? Because biting into a juicy chicken drumstick that's coated in crispy, spicy batter is fantastic! There's a reason many people order them at restaurants but don't make them at home: it's easy for excellent homemade batter to be ruined by dry meat if you overcook the chicken. By precooking the chicken sous vide, you won't lose all that moisture by deep-frying the chicken for too long. All it needs is a quick flash in really hot oil to crisp the batter.

SPICY SOUTHERN-FRIED CHICKEN

🌡 150°F/66°C | ⏱ 2 HOURS | 🍴 SERVES 4 (ABOUT 8 PIECES)

Note: Although the sous vide element only takes 2 hours, if you're brining the chicken in my lemon brine first, you need to start this the night before, or in the morning.

INGREDIENTS

LEMON BRINE

1 quart/1 L water

¼ cup/62 g salt

2 tablespoons/60 ml honey

1 garlic clove, smashed

3 bay leaves

½ tablespoon/7 g black pepper

5 sprigs thyme

5 sprigs parsley

1 sprig rosemary

Zest and juice of ½ a lemon

CHICKEN

2 pounds/900 g chicken legs and thighs, separated

Vegetable or peanut oil, for deep frying

EGG WASH

3 eggs, beaten

1 cup/240 ml hot sauce

FLOUR COATING

2 cups/240 g self-rising flour

2 teaspoons ground fresh rosemary

1 tablespoon/15 g Cajun seasoning

2 teaspoons/10 g garlic powder

1 teaspoon/5 g ground black pepper

1 teaspoon/5 g salt

DIRECTIONS

To make the brine, combine all of the brine ingredients in a large bowl and whisk well to blend. Submerge the chicken in the brine, then cover the bowl and refrigerate 8 hours or overnight.

Note: The brining process is not essential, but it does add some great flavor, tenderizes the chicken, and works well to help it retain extra moisture during sous vide cooking.

When you're ready to cook the chicken, preheat a sous vide water bath to 155°F/68°C.

Gently rinse off the brine mixture with cool water, shake off the excess water, and seal the chicken pieces in vacuum-seal bags. You should be able to fit about 4 pieces per bag. Cook in the preheated water bath for 2 hours. When the chicken has finished cooking sous vide, cut open the vacuum-seal bags, drain any liquid (you may want to reserve this liquid for a delicious chicken stock), and set the chicken aside.

While the chicken rests, pour at least 4 inches/10 cm of oil into a deep fryer or a pot and heat to 400°F/204°C.

To make the egg wash, combine the eggs and hot sauce in a medium-size bowl.

To make the flour coating, combine all the ingredients in a large bowl.

Coat the chicken pieces by dipping them in the egg wash and then rolling them in the flour coating in batches of 3 or 4. Deep-fry each batch until the chicken is golden and crispy. Check the chicken regularly as this should only take a few minutes—remember, the chicken is already cooked, so you're just looking for the perfect crisp on the skin. You can rest the cooked pieces on a wire rack while you fry the rest, or serve the chicken in batches as they are ready.

I've found this sous vide chicken breast goes great with tangy, sweet honey mustard sauce. I recommend serving it with this pea- and corn-studded sweet potato mash, but it also plates well with loads of other veggies—asparagus, for example. The chicken breast is juicy because it's been cooked until just-done, which makes it perfect for mopping up the sauce. If you find this honey mustard sauce as delicious as I do, you'll have a hard time stopping yourself from eating half of it before the chicken's ready!

HONEY MUSTARD CHICKEN WITH SWEET POTATO MASH

✳ 140°F/60°C | ⏱ 1¼ HOURS | ✗ SERVES 4

INGREDIENTS

4 boneless, skinless chicken breasts

Sea salt and freshly ground pepper

4 tablespoons/56 g unsalted butter, divided

HONEY MUSTARD SAUCE

¼ cup/60 ml honey

2 tablespoons/30 ml distilled white vinegar

2 tablespoons/30 g Dijon mustard

2 tablespoons/30 g whole-grain mustard

2 garlic cloves

2 tablespoons/30 ml extra-virgin olive oil

2 tablespoons/30 ml water

SWEET POTATO MASH

4 sweet potatoes, peeled and chopped into ½-inch/1 cm chunks

2 tablespoons/28 g unsalted butter

2 tablespoons/30 g heavy cream

Sea salt and black pepper

½ cup/80 g fresh or frozen peas, cooked and drained

½ cup/82 g sweet corn, cooked and drained

DIRECTIONS

Preheat a sous vide water bath to 140°F/60°C.

Seal the chicken breasts in vacuum-seal bags, either 1 or 2 breasts per bag depending on the size of your bags, and cook in the preheated water bath for 1 hour 15 minutes.

To make the sauce, whisk together the sauce ingredients in a medium-size bowl. Cover and set aside.

When the chicken has 30 minutes left to cook, make the sweet potato mash. Bring a pot of water to a boil, add the sweet potato chunks to the water, and boil until tender, around 10 to 12 minutes. Drain the water and mash the potatoes in a large bowl (or mash them right in the cooking pot) with the butter, heavy cream, and salt and pepper to taste. Mix the cooked peas and corn into the mash, stirring to combine, then cover the bowl to keep warm.

When the chicken breasts are done, take them out of the vacuum-seal bags and discard any liquid from the bags. Pat the chicken breasts dry with paper towels and season with salt and pepper. Heat a frying pan over high heat until it starts to smoke, add 2 tablespoons of the butter, and sear the chicken breasts for 1 minute on each side, then set them aside on a cutting board. Turn the heat down to medium and pour the honey mustard sauce into the frying pan to deglaze it. Stir continuously for 10 to 20 seconds before pouring it back into the bowl (don't reduce the sauce too much or it will become too thick and gloopy).

Spoon the mash onto each of 4 plates. Slice the chicken and arrange it on top of the mash, then drizzle the honey mustard sauce over the top.

Steak tartare is such a classic starter that I'd feel blasphemous to the beef gods if I changed it too much. We certainly won't be cooking the steak sous vide! That means the main difference between this recipe and your "classic" steak tartare is the addition of a sous vide egg yolk. Instead of running thinly when broken, this yolk oozes. It's satisfying to break and clings to the beef really well. I've also added lemon juice to the dressing, which gives the dish a bit of brightness. Please note, however, that you should only add the lemon right at the very end before serving. Otherwise, the lemon's acidity may start to "cook" the beef.

STEAK TARTARE WITH SOUS VIDE EGG YOLK

🌡* 144°F/62°C | ⏲ 1 HOUR | 🍴 SERVES 4 AS A STARTER

INGREDIENTS

½ cup/120 ml plus 1 tablespoon olive oil, divided

4 egg yolks (you may want to make extra in case any break—they are quite delicate!)

10 ounces/280 g beef tenderloin or sirloin, fat trimmed

1½ teaspoons/8 ml Worcestershire sauce

1½ teaspoons/7 g ketchup

1 tablespoon/14 g Dijon mustard

Sea salt and black pepper

1 teaspoon/5 ml Tabasco or red pepper flakes (optional)

¼ cup/40 g diced shallot (about 2 small shallots)

1 tablespoon/8 g finely diced drained capers and 1 tablespoon/15 ml caper vinegar, plus 1 teaspoon/3 g whole capers to garnish

1 tablespoon/5 g finely sliced fresh chives, plus 8 full chives to garnish

1 tablespoon/15 ml freshly squeezed lemon juice

Crostini, to serve

DIRECTIONS

Preheat a sous vide water bath to 144°F/62°C.

Pour ½ cup/120 ml olive oil into a resealable plastic bag and carefully place the egg yolks in the bag. Submerge the bag in the preheated water bath using the displacement method (see page 14), clip the bag to the side of the preheated water bath, and cook for 1 hour.

After 30 minutes of the cooking time has passed, transfer the beef from the fridge to the freezer to firm up. This is also a good time to place 4 plates in the freezer for serving.

About 5 to 10 minutes before the eggs have finished cooking sous vide, prepare the tartare (don't worry about leaving the eggs in the water bath for a few extra minutes if you run a little long on time). Take the steak out of the freezer and finely dice with a sharp chef's knife.

In a large bowl, whisk together the remaining 1 tablespoon olive oil, Worcestershire sauce, ketchup, Dijon mustard, salt and pepper to taste, and Tabasco. Then stir in the shallots, finely diced capers, caper vinegar, sliced chives, and the finely diced beef and stir well to combine. Lastly, just before serving, stir in the freshly squeezed lemon juice.

Remove the plates from the freezer and divide the mixture into 4 servings, forming the beef into patties on the plates and leaving a slight indent in the center to hold the slippery egg yolk (you can use a burger ring or similar tool to help shape the patties).

One by one, carefully remove the egg yolks from the bag and very gently place one on top of each plate of beef tartare. Season the eggs with a touch of salt. Garnish by arranging some capers and the chives over each plate, and serve with crostini.

This recipe is one of the few in this book that use jars rather than bags for the sous vide bath. I've found it's a fun technique for savory and sweet dishes alike. The key ingredients in this creamy pâté are the chicken livers, fresh herbs, and bourbon whiskey. While you can make four (or more) to serve a group, I've found this is also a nice recipe for impressing a date: you can just halve the ingredients. Serve with crusty bread or crackers.

CHICKEN LIVER PÂTÉ POTS

♨* 155°F/68°C | ⌛ 1½ HOURS | ✗ SERVES 4

INGREDIENTS

1 tablespoon/14 g unsalted butter

2 shallots, finely diced

2 garlic cloves, minced

¼ cup/60 ml bourbon whiskey

1 teaspoon thyme leaves

1 teaspoon rosemary leaves

8 ounces/230 g chicken livers, trimmed

1 egg plus 1 egg yolk

Salt and black pepper

2 tablespoons/28 g unsalted butter, melted

Note: For this recipe you'll need either 2 8-ounce/240 ml wide-mouth canning jars so each jar holds 2 servings, or 4 4-ounce/120 ml wide-mouth canning jars for individual servings.

DIRECTIONS

Preheat a sous vide water bath to 155°F/68°C.

Melt the 1 tablespoon butter in a frying pan over medium-low heat. Add the shallots and garlic and fry for 15 minutes, or until the shallots are softened, stirring frequently. Turn the heat up to medium and pour the bourbon into the frying pan along with the thyme and rosemary, and cook for 3 minutes to allow some of the alcohol to burn off, making sure you scrape any bits off the bottom of the frying pan so they combine with the sauce.

Transfer the contents of the pan to a food processor along with chicken livers, egg, egg yolk, and salt and black pepper to taste and process for 3 to 4 minutes, or until very smooth. Transfer the blended mixture to the jars, seal the lids, and carefully place into the sous vide water bath (lidded side up) with tongs and a spatula. Cook in the preheated water bath for 1½ hours.

When the pâté has finished cooking, remove the jars from the water bath and allow them to cool on the counter for 5 minutes (this step helps prevent the glass from cracking). Once they cool slightly, plunge them into an ice water bath for 5 to 10 minutes. Remove the lids, pour off any liquid from the surface, scrape off the top layer that has oxidized, and pour some melted butter over the top. Put the lids back on and refrigerate for a minimum of 3 hours, or overnight. Although you can eat the pâté after 3 hours, if you leave it in the fridge for a day or two the flavors will continue to meld and develop.

CHAPTER 4
SALADS AND SMALL BITES

This earthy recipe is perfect for anyone bored of leafy green salads. It features creamy goat cheese, crunchy walnuts, and a hint of sourness from the semi-pickled beets. Wait, pickled beets in one day? Yes, by using sous vide, you can have pickled beets on hand in just over an hour!

BEET AND GOAT CHEESE SALAD

🌡 194°F/90°C | ⏲ 1¼ HOURS | 🍴 SERVES 4

INGREDIENTS

PICKLING BRINE

½ cup/120 ml white wine vinegar

¼ cup/60 ml water

3 tablespoons/38 g sugar

1 teaspoon salt

½ teaspoon/2½ g mustard powder

5 black peppercorns

3 cloves

SALAD

2 beets, peeled, trimmed, and chopped into ½-inch/1-cm cubes

2 cups/60 g arugula

2 cups/60 g watercress

½ cup/25 g roughly chopped mint leaves

½ cup/56 g loosely crumbled goat cheese

½ cup/56 g walnuts, toasted and roughly chopped

LEMON BASIL DRESSING

¼ cup/60 ml extra-virgin oil

1 tablespoon/15 ml lemon juice

1 tablespoon/15 ml white wine vinegar

1 tablespoon/6 g finely chopped fresh basil

½ teaspoon/10 g Dijon mustard

1 garlic clove, minced

¼ teaspoon/1⅔ g sea salt

¼ teaspoon/1⅔ g black pepper

DIRECTIONS

To make the pickling brine, combine all the brine ingredients in a resealable plastic bag, seal, and shake.

Place the beets in the pickling brine. I recommend you do this before you turn on your sous vide machine to give the beets some extra time in the pickling liquid.

Preheat a sous vide water bath to 194°F/90°C; it helps to cover the water bath with tin foil (if it doesn't already have a lid) to help the water heat up faster.

Place the bag containing the beets into the water bath and seal using the displacement method (see page 14), clip the bag to the edge of the preheated water bath, and cook for 1 hour 15 minutes.

Meanwhile, to make the dressing, combine all the dressing ingredients in a jar and shake to blend (alternatively, you can combine them in a small bowl, stir well, and cover). Store the dressing in the fridge until ready to use.

When the beets have finished cooking sous vide, remove the bag from the sous vide water bath and plunge it into an ice water bath for 10 minutes. Once the beets have thoroughly cooled, combine the arugula, watercress, and mint leaves in a large bowl and toss with the dressing until well coated (give the dressing another good shake before pouring it on). Then toss in the goat cheese and walnuts.

If you're serving the beets immediately, open the bag containing the beets and remove them from the liquid with a slotted spoon. Pick out any peppercorns and cloves, then toss the beets with the salad. If you want to keep some of the beets for another day, transfer them to a jar or container with enough liquid from the bag to cover the beets.

Thai food is about so much more than just pad Thai and curries. In fact, the realm of Thai salads is a whole different culinary area unto itself. For me, you just can't beat a tangy Thai salad dressing, made from a perfectly balanced combination of lime juice, fish sauce, and palm sugar. Although I've used green mango in this salad, you can also make it with green papaya, green apple, or even carrots. In Thailand, they often put up to five garlic cloves per person in a mango salad, which may be a bit overwhelming for some. I've reduced the quantity to one or two cloves per person in this recipe, but if you're adventurous, go ahead and add more!

GREEN MANGO SALAD WITH SHRIMP

♨ 135°F/57°C | ⏱ 15 MINUTES | 🍴 SERVES 4

INGREDIENTS

SALAD

24 medium-size shrimp, peeled and deveined

4 green (unripe) mangoes, peeled and shredded on a mandoline, cut with a zigzag peeler, or sliced into thin strips with a knife

2 medium shallots, thinly sliced

¾ cup/150 g cherry tomatoes, halved

2 tablespoons/12½ g chopped fresh Thai basil leaves (or regular basil if you can't find Thai basil)

¼ cup/35 g peanuts, toasted in a dry pan

THAI DRESSING

¼ cup/60 ml freshly squeezed lime juice

6 tablespoons/69 g palm sugar or firmly packed light brown sugar

6 tablespoons/30 ml fish sauce

4 to 8 garlic cloves, or to taste

4 to 8 small red chiles, or to taste

DIRECTIONS

Preheat a sous vide water bath to 135°F/57°C.

Arrange the shrimp so that they are lying flat and in a single layer in vacuum-seal bags. Seal and cook in the preheated water bath for 15 minutes.

To make the dressing, in a small bowl, mix together the lime juice, palm sugar, and fish sauce and whisk until well combined. Pound the garlic with a mortar and pestle, then add the chiles and continue to pound. With a spoon, loosen the chile and garlic from the mortar with about a ¼ cup/60 ml of the dressing, then combine the mixture with the rest of the dressing. Set aside.

When the shrimp has finished cooking sous vide, remove the bag from the sous vide water bath and set aside on the counter.

In a large bowl, combine the green mango strips with the shallots, tomato halves, Thai basil, and peanuts. Cut open the bags containing the shrimp, drain and discard any liquid, and add the shrimp to the salad. Pour the dressing over the salad and toss to combine. Serve immediately.

In this salad, cheese and nuts accent pear slices that have been infused with a hint of honey while they cook sous vide. The pear will soften slightly during cooking, but you'll find it will still have a good bit of crunch to it.

PEAR, PARMESAN, AND WALNUT SALAD

🌡 159°F/70°C | ⏱ 30 MINUTES | 🍴 SERVES 4

INGREDIENTS

SALAD

2 tablespoons/60 ml honey

2 pears, cored, halved, and thinly sliced

½ cup/56 g walnuts, lightly toasted and roughly chopped

½ cup/50 g shaved Parmesan

4 cups/120 g arugula

Sea salt and black pepper

GARLIC DIJON DRESSING

¼ cup/60 ml olive oil

1 tablespoon/15 ml white wine vinegar

1 teaspoon/5 g Dijon mustard

1 garlic clove, minced

Salt to taste

DIRECTIONS

Preheat a sous vide water bath to 159°F/71°C.

Pour the honey into a heat-proof bowl and heat in the microwave for about 20 seconds, or until the honey loosens up. Toss the pear slices in the honey and lay them flat in vacuum-seal bags (as many bags as is needed to have each pear slice flat, side by side).

Seal and cook in the preheated water bath for 30 minutes. Plunge the bags into an ice water bath for 5 to 10 minutes and then chill in the fridge for at least 3 hours (or overnight).

Meanwhile, to make the dressing, mix the dressing ingredients together in a jar, shake to combine, and then store the dressing in the fridge until you're ready to use it (the flavors will develop over time).

Before serving, cut open the bag containing the pears and drain any liquid. To serve, combine the walnuts, Parmesan, and arugula in a large bowl. Add the drained pear slices, then the dressing, toss together, and taste the salad. Season with salt and pepper.

The zingy Thai dressing in this recipe features loads of herbs. I think you'll find it's as good as any you'd order in a Thai restaurant. The other reason people love ordering this dish out is the crazy tender beef. With sous vide, you can recreate that right at home.

SPICY THAI BEEF SALAD

🌡 129°F/54°C | ⏱ 2 HOURS | 🍴 SERVES 4

INGREDIENTS

SALAD

1 pound/450 g beef tenderloin

Salt and pepper

2 tablespoons/30 ml vegetable oil

1 cup/200 g cherry tomatoes, halved

1 red onion, finely sliced

½ cup/25 g cilantro leaves, torn

½ cup/25 g mint leaves, torn

½ cup/25 g fresh Thai basil leaves (or regular basil if you can't find Thai basil), torn

⅓ cup/46 g peanuts, toasted and roughly chopped

2 kaffir lime leaves, very finely sliced (optional)

SPICY THAI DRESSING

6 tablespoons/90 ml fish sauce

¼ cup/60 ml lime juice

1 tablespoon/12 g palm sugar or firmly packed light brown sugar

4 garlic cloves

2 small red chiles, stems trimmed

DIRECTIONS

Preheat a sous vide water bath to 129°F/54°C.

Seal the beef tenderloin in a vacuum-seal bag and cook in the preheated water bath for 2 hours.

While the beef is cooking, whisk together the fish sauce, lime juice, and sugar in a medium-size bowl. Pound the garlic and chiles into a coarse mixture with a mortar and pestle. With a spoon, loosen the garlic and chile mixture from the mortar with about ¼ cup/60 ml of the dressing, then combine the mixture with the rest of the dressing. Cover and refrigerate.

When the beef has finished cooking sous vide, remove it from the bag and pat it dry. Generously season with salt and pepper. Heat a frying pan over high heat until it's smoking hot. Add the vegetable oil and fry the beef for 1 to 1½ minutes on each side, or until you get a good sear (try to do this as quickly as possible to stop the steak from overcooking!). Set the steak aside on a chopping board and let it rest.

In a large bowl, combine the cherry tomatoes, red onion, cilantro, mint, Thai basil, peanuts, and kaffir lime leaves. Slice the steak very thinly with a sharp chef's knife and add it to the bowl. Pour the dressing over the salad and toss to combine. Serve immediately.

Deep-fried eggs often fall into two categories: the yolk is either very soft and runs all over your plate, or it's hard (like in a Scotch egg). I wanted to create an egg that was gooey, but still firm, to star in this dish. Because sous vide eggs are quite delicate, you may want to make a few extra in case they break. In this recipe, I cook the eggs at 167°F/75°C for 13 minutes instead of at 147°F/64°C for 45 minutes like I recommend elsewhere so that the egg whites are firmer—it will help them withstand the handling.

PANKO EGGS ON SALAD NIÇOISE

🌡 167°F/75°C | 🕐 13 MINUTES | 🍴 SERVES 4

INGREDIENTS

PANKO EGGS

8 or more extra-large eggs, at room temperature (this is important!)

1 cup/50 g panko bread crumbs

1 cup/100 g grated Parmesan cheese

Sea salt and black pepper

Vegetable or canola oil, for deep frying

1 cup/120 g flour

2 eggs, beaten with 2 tablespoons water

SHALLOT DIJON DRESSING

6 tablespoons/90 ml olive oil

¼ cup/60 ml white wine vinegar

4 teaspoons/20 g Dijon mustard

1 shallot, minced

Salt and black pepper

NIÇOISE SALAD

2 heads butterhead lettuce, leaves separated, torn

2 cups/60g watercress

2 handfuls cherry tomatoes, halved

1¼ cups/125 g pitted black olives

2 cups/250 g green beans, boiled for 1½ minutes, chopped into 1-inch/2-cm segments

3 tablespoons/24 g drained capers

20 anchovies

Salt and black pepper

DIRECTIONS

Preheat a sous vide water bath to 167°F/75°C.

To make the eggs, use a spatula to carefully lower the eggs directly into the preheated water bath (if you just drop them in they may crack). Cook sous vide for 13 minutes.

While the eggs cook, make the dressing. Combine all of the dressing ingredients in a bowl and mix well to combine. Cover and refrigerate.

Prepare the rest of the salad by combining the lettuce, watercress, tomatoes, olives, green beans, and capers in a large bowl. Set aside.

Heat 4 inches/10 cm of vegetable oil in a pot over high heat to 360°F/182°C. While it heats, combine the bread crumbs, Parmesan, salt, and pepper in a small bowl. Make sure to crunch up any large bread crumb pieces with your hands to make the texture more uniform. Place the flour into another small bowl and make sure the beaten egg mixture is ready in a third small bowl.

When the eggs have finished cooking sous vide, take them out and transfer them to an ice water bath until they are cool enough for you to peel them.

NOW FOLLOW THESE STEPS FOR EACH EGG ONE AT A TIME:

1. Carefully peel away enough eggshell so that the egg can slip out of the shell and onto your hand without breaking the yolk.

2. While the egg is still in your hand, carefully dust the whole egg with flour, spoon over the beaten egg mixture until it's coated all over, and coat the egg in bread crumbs, gently packing them down against the egg to ensure good coverage.

3. Carefully drop the eggs into the hot oil (only do this when the oil has reached temperature). Deep-fry until nicely golden, about 30 seconds. Turn the egg carefully with a spatula during cooking to ensure even browning.

4. Once the egg is golden brown, take it out of the oil and place it on paper towels.

5. Repeat these steps with the remaining eggs.

Pour the dressing over the salad and toss to combine. Serve the salad topped with the anchovies and eggs.

Nutty, refreshing, and just a little bit sweet from the maple-infused apple slices, this salad will keep you coming back bite after bite. The lemon, parsley, and yogurt dressing makes it the perfect summer salad.

WALDORF SALAD WITH MAPLE-INFUSED APPLE SLICES

🌡 159°F/71°C | ⏲ 30 MINUTES | 🍴 SERVES 4

INGREDIENTS

SALAD

¼ cup/160 ml maple syrup

2 green apples, cored, quartered, and thinly sliced

1½ cups/150 g thinly sliced celery

1½ cups/225 g seedless red grapes, halved

1½ cups/170 g walnuts, lightly toasted

2 heads leafy lettuce, such as butterhead, leaves removed

LEMON, PARSLEY, AND YOGURT DRESSING

½ cup/113 g plain yogurt

2 tablespoons/30 g mayonnaise

1 tablespoon/15 ml lemon juice

1 tablespoon/ 6¼ g finely chopped fresh parsley

1 tablespoon/ 6¼ g finely chopped fresh mint

1 teaspoon/3 ml maple syrup

DIRECTIONS

Preheat a sous vide water bath to 159°F/71°C.

In a small bowl, microwave the maple syrup in a heat-proof bowl for 20 seconds. Toss the apple slices in the syrup to coat. Place the apple slices in vacuum-seal bags, using as many bags as necessary to lay them flat in single layers, and then spoon any excess maple syrup into the bags and seal. Cook the apple slices in the preheated water bath for 30 minutes. Plunge the bags into an ice water bath and transfer the bath to the freezer for 10 minutes to help the apples cool as quickly as possible.

To make the dressing, combine all the dressing ingredients in a large bowl. Stir well to combine, then cover and refrigerate.

Remove the bags from the freezer, cut them open, and tip the apple slices onto a plate. In a large bowl, toss the celery, grapes, and walnuts in the dressing, then gently fold in the apple slices. Serve the salad on top of the lettuce leaves.

Everybody loves a good Caesar salad, but all too often the dry, overcooked chicken seems like an afterthought. Luckily with sous vide, you're guaranteed tender, moist chicken every time. My Caesar dressing is creamy but also has plenty of acidity to cut through and keep it bright. Feel free to leave out the anchovies if they aren't your thing or add extra Parmesan on top if you're a cheese lover!

CHICKEN CAESAR SALAD

🌡* 140°F/60°C | ⏲ 1¼ HOURS | 🍴 SERVES 4

SALAD

2 chicken breasts

Sea salt and freshly ground pepper

¼ cup/60 ml vegetable oil

1 garlic clove, halved

1 medium-size ciabatta loaf, sliced ½ inch/1-cm thick

4 romaine hearts, chopped

CAESAR DRESSING

2 tablespoons/30 ml white vinegar

2 tablespoons/30 ml lemon juice

4 egg yolks

1 teaspoon/14 g Dijon mustard

½ cup/120 ml olive oil

⅔ cup/66 g finely grated Parmesan

12 anchovy fillets, minced

2 garlic cloves, minced

Sea salt and freshly ground pepper

DIRECTIONS

Preheat a sous vide water bath to 140°F/60°C.

Seal each chicken breast in a vacuum-seal bag and cook in the preheated water bath for 1 hour 15 minutes.

While the chicken cooks, mix together all of the dressing ingredients in a medium-size bowl. Cover and refrigerate.

When the chicken is done, cut open the vacuum-seal bags, discarding the liquid in the bags, pat the breasts dry with paper towels, and season with salt and pepper. Heat a frying pan over high heat, add the vegetable oil, and sear the chicken on both sides until just browned, 1 to 2 minutes. Set the chicken aside on a cutting board to rest. Leave the frying pan on the heat and move on to the next step immediately.

Rub the garlic clove over both sides of the bread and sprinkle with salt and pepper. Fry the bread slices in the hot oil until nicely browned, flipping halfway through. Remove the bread from the pan and set aside.

In a large bowl, toss the lettuce in the dressing, then divide among 4 serving bowls. Slice the chicken and top each bowl with about half a chicken breast. Roughly chop the bread and scatter the resulting croutons over the top.

Although this is not a sous vide recipe, if you have a vacuum sealer, you have to give it a try. These vibrant red, compressed watermelon cubes will feel like they're bursting in your mouth—the fun of summer in a bite! This light and colorful salad features a good amount of cheese to ensure you're not left hungry. (It also goes great with the Rosemary and Garlic Rack of Lamb on page 89.)

COMPRESSED WATERMELON SALAD WITH FETA AND MINT

✖ SERVES 4

SALAD

½ medium-size watermelon (around 5 to 6 cups/750 to 900 g), chopped into ½- to ¾-inch/1- to 2-cm cubes

1 cup/30 g arugula

1 cup/30 g watercress

1 cup/50 g mint leaves, finely chopped

½ cup/56 g crumbled feta

SHALLOT AND LEMON DRESSING

¼ cup/60 ml extra-virgin olive oil

1 tablespoon/30 ml lemon juice

1 tablespoon/30 ml white wine vinegar

1 tablespoon/10 g finely diced shallot

1 garlic clove, minced

½ teaspoon lemon zest

1 teaspoon/5 ml honey

DIRECTIONS

To make the salad, seal the watermelon cubes in 1 or 2 vacuum-seal bags, depending on the size of your bags and watermelon, and place in the fridge for a minimum of 3 hours.

Note: A chamber vacuum sealer (pages 15 to 16) is needed to make perfectly compressed watermelon, but a regular vacuum sealer will get you most of the way there.

To make the dressing, combine all of the dressing ingredients in a food processor and blend for 1 minute. Store the dressing in the fridge until you're ready to use it.

Combine the arugula, watercress, mint, and feta in a large bowl and toss well with the shallot and lemon dressing. Divide among 4 plates. Cut open the sous vide bag and arrange the watermelon on top of the salad. Season with salt and pepper to taste.

The idea behind this side dish is to allow the humble carrot to really shine. To that end, the carrots are shaved into ribbons and coated in butter and honey and accented only with thyme. This is a vegetable dish sure to please even the most carnivorous of friends—and it looks really good, too! You could also use fingerling carrots for this recipe, but slice them in half so that they cook through.

HONEY-GLAZED CARROTS

♨ 185°F/85°C | ⏱ 20 MINUTES | 🍴 SERVES 4 TO 6 AS A SIDE DISH

INGREDIENTS

8 tablespoons/113 g unsalted butter, melted

2 tablespoons/30 ml honey

Sea salt and pepper to taste

4 medium carrots, shaved into ribbons with a mandoline or vegetable peeler

8 sprigs fresh thyme

DIRECTIONS

Preheat a sous vide water bath to 185°F/85°C.

Combine the melted butter, honey, and salt and pepper to taste in a mixing bowl and stir to combine. Gently toss the carrot ribbons in the glaze.

Transfer the glazed carrots to vacuum-seal bags (reserving the excess glaze for later). Lay them as flat as possible within the bag. Place the thyme sprigs on top, then seal. Cook in the preheated water bath for 20 minutes.

Cut open the bag and arrange the carrots on a large serving plate along with a few of the thyme sprigs. Drizzle some of the reserved glaze over the top, season with salt and pepper to taste, and serve.

Say good-bye to washed-out, limp asparagus spears. Cook them sous vide, cover them in butter, garlic, and a sprinkling of salt, and you'll be in side-dish heaven. With this cooking time, asparagus has a good amount of crunch left in it and retains its vibrant green.

ASPARAGUS HALVES WITH CRISPY GARLIC CHIPS

🌡 185°F/85°C | ⏱ 15 MINUTES | 🍴 SERVES 4 AS A SIDE DISH

INGREDIENTS

1 pound/450 g asparagus spears

⅓ cup/75 g unsalted butter, melted

Sea salt and black pepper

5 garlic cloves, minced

1 cup/240 ml vegetable oil

15 garlic cloves, finely sliced

DIRECTIONS

Preheat a sous vide water bath to 185°F/85°C.

Peel the asparagus stalks with a vegetable peeler and halve them lengthwise.

In a small baking dish or on a plate, combine the melted butter and salt and black pepper to taste, then roll the asparagus halves in the mixture until they're well coated (reserve the remaining butter for later). Transfer the asparagus to vacuum-seal bags, using as many as necessary to arrange them side by side in a single layer. Add the 5 minced garlic cloves to the bags, seal, and cook in the preheated water bath for 15 minutes.

Meanwhile, heat the vegetable oil in a small pot to 350°F/177°C. Add the 15 finely sliced garlic cloves and fry until browned, about 2 minutes, then drain on paper towels.

Cut open the sous vide bags and tip the contents out onto a serving plate, drizzle over a bit of the leftover butter that you reserved, and top with the crispy garlic. Season with additional salt and black pepper to taste.

This pea purée is bright from the mint and creamy from the addition of crème fraîche and butter. If you want to make it even richer, you can substitute cream for the crème fraîche.

MINTED PEA PURÉE

🌡* 185°F/85°C | ⏱ 45 MINUTES | 🍴 SERVES 4

INGREDIENTS

1 package (16 ounces/450 g) frozen peas, thawed

1 tablespoon/14 g unsalted butter

1 garlic clove, chopped

¼ cup/12 g fresh mint leaves

2 tablespoons/30 g crème fraîche

Sea salt and white pepper to taste

DIRECTIONS

Preheat a sous vide water bath to 185°F/85°C.

Combine the peas, butter, garlic, and mint in a resealable bag and submerge using the displacement method (see page 14), clip the bag to the side of the preheated water bath, and cook for 45 minutes.

Remove the bag from the water bath. Transfer the contents to a food processor or blender and add the crème fraîche. Process until smooth and add salt and pepper to taste. Serve immediately.

Sure, you can steam your corn and then butter it—it's not that hard. But with sous vide, you get to really immerse the corn in buttery goodness. (Don't worry—even though you cook the corn in the butter, it won't absorb anywhere near all of it!) The cooking process also lends itself to additional flavorings. In this recipe, I've used a few of my favorite herbs, but feel free to mix it up, or keep it simple with just butter. Or, if you have some of the herb-infused butter from page 274 in the fridge, you can use that!

HERB-INFUSED CORN ON THE COB

🌡 185°F/85°C | ⏱ 35 MINUTES | 🍴 SERVES 4

INGREDIENTS

1 cup/226 g unsalted butter, melted

1 tablespoon/6 g finely chopped fresh parsley

1 tablespoon/5 g finely chopped fresh chives

1 tablespoon/9 g finely chopped garlic

4 ears corn

Salt and black pepper to taste

DIRECTIONS

Preheat a sous vide water bath to 185°F/85°C.

Combine the melted butter, parsley, chives, and garlic in a medium-size bowl and whisk to blend. Seal each ear of corn individually with one-fourth of the butter mixture in each vacuum-seal bag. Cook in the preheated water bath for 35 minutes. You may need to weight the bags down with something (I use large glass mugs, for example, simply placing them on top of the corn to keep them under water) because they can float to the surface!

Remove the corn from the bag and serve immediately, seasoned with salt and black pepper. You can pour the extra butter sauce into a gravy boat or other serving dish for anyone who wants extra butter.

These potato pots are made with thinly sliced potatoes so you can get some good layering in the ramekins. With ample creamy and cheesy flavors along with a hint of cayenne, this dish is satisfyingly filling but has a little kick, which you can tailor to your preference. Sous vide ensures that you get perfectly cooked potatoes every time.

MINI SCALLOPED POTATO POTS

🌡 185°F/85°C | ⏱ 2 HOURS | 🍴 SERVES 6

INGREDIENTS

1½ pounds/680 g new potatoes, 1½ to 2 inches/4 to 5 cm wide, peeled and sliced ⅛ inch/3 mm thick (a mandoline is ideal for this if you have one)

¾ cup/170 g unsalted butter, melted

1 cup/240 ml heavy cream

1 cup/240 g crème fraîche

Pinch of cayenne

Salt and black pepper to taste

6 tablespoons/84 g grated sharp Cheddar cheese

Note: For this recipe you'll need 6- to 8-ounce/180- to 240-ml ramekins, one per person.

DIRECTIONS

Preheat a sous vide water bath to 185°F/85°C.

Arrange the potatoes in single layers in 2 vacuum-seal bags, each with half of the melted butter. Cook in the preheated water bath for 2 hours.

With about 10 minutes left on the potatoes, preheat the oven to 400°F/200°C.

When the potatoes have finished cooking sous vide, remove the bags from the water bath and set aside on a cutting board to cool a little. Meanwhile, whisk together the cream, crème fraîche, cayenne, and salt and pepper to taste in a medium-size bowl. Cut open the vacuum-seal bags and brush the insides of the ramekins with some of the melted butter in the bags. Layer the potatoes in the buttered ramekins (discarding any excess butter), whisk the cream mixture to recombine, and pour evenly over the ramekins. Sprinkle 1 tablespoon of cheese over each, place the ramekins on a baking sheet, and bake for 10 to 20 minutes, or until the cheese is golden brown.

Many people get put off making their own hummus because they find it difficult to get the consistency right and end up with a grainy, lumpy dip. This recipe keeps it reasonably simple and authentic(ish) by calling for dried chickpeas. While gauging the water quantity when you're cooking them in a pot on the stove top can be tricky, sous vide ensures you can walk away during the cooking time and come back to cooked chickpeas that are ready to go.

HUMMUS WITH LEMON AND TAHINI

✴ 194°F/90°C | 🕐 3¼ HOURS | 🍴 SERVES 4 TO 6 AS AN APPETIZER, MAKES ABOUT 1 CUP

INGREDIENTS

¾ cup/150 g dried chickpeas

5 cups/1,190 ml water, for soaking

2 cups/475 ml plus 2 tablespoons water, for cooking

3 tablespoons/42 g tahini

3 garlic cloves, crushed

3 tablespoons/45 ml freshly squeezed lemon juice (about 1 lemon)

5 tablespoons/75 ml good-quality extra-virgin olive oil, plus extra to serve

Pinch of paprika, to serve

Chopped cilantro, to serve

DIRECTIONS

In a container with a lid, combine the chickpeas and 5 cups/1,190 ml soaking water. Soak for 12 hours in the fridge.

The next day (or 12 hours later), preheat a sous vide water bath to 194°F/90°C.

Drain the soaked chickpeas, discarding the soaking water. Combine the chickpeas and water for cooking in a resealable plastic bag. Submerge in the preheated water bath using the displacement method (see page 14), clip the bag to the side of the preheated water bath, and cook for 3 hours 15 minutes.

Drain the chickpeas in a colander or sieve. Transfer the chickpeas to a blender, reserving about 1 tablespoon whole chickpeas for garnish, and add the tahini, garlic, lemon juice, and extra-virgin olive oil. Pulse until smooth but still with some texture; you don't want to get it to the point that it's perfectly uniform.

Transfer the dip to a serving bowl, making a circular depression in the center with the back of a spoon. Dust with paprika and drizzle over ample extra-virgin olive oil, letting it pool in the center. Then scatter the reserved chickpeas on top along with the cilantro. Serve with pita bread, crackers, bread, or carrot and celery sticks.

This recipe starts with sous vide shrimp in a chile and garlic sauce, and then it hits them with a blast from a blowtorch! Torching the shrimp allows you to get maximum char with minimum risk of overcooking. It's a great way to make sure the shrimp stay at their optimum temperature while also picking up some great smoky flavors. If you don't have a blowtorch and aren't interested in getting one, you can always finish the shrimp off on the grill or in a very hot frying pan—but bear in mind they are very easy to overcook!

TORCHED SHRIMP WITH CHILE AND GARLIC

🌡 135°F/57°C | 🕐 15 MINUTES | 🍴 MAKES 4 SKEWERS

INGREDIENTS

12 large shrimp, peeled and deveined, tail on

12 garlic cloves, minced

2 teaspoons/3.6 g red pepper flakes, plus more to serve

¼ cup/60 ml olive oil, plus more to serve

2 teaspoons/10 ml white vinegar

2 tablespoons/30 ml hot sauce

Sea salt and freshly ground black pepper

1 lemon, cut into wedges

DIRECTIONS

Preheat a sous vide water bath to 135°F/57°C.

Lay the shrimp flat and seal in vacuum-seal bags. Cook in the preheated water bath for 15 minutes.

Meanwhile, in a small bowl, mix together the garlic, red pepper flakes, olive oil, vinegar, hot sauce, and salt and pepper to taste.

Remove the shrimp from the bag, discarding any liquid, and toss them in the sauce. Thread 3 shrimp onto each of 4 skewers, spearing them through the top and tail (as in the photo).

Char the shrimp with the blowtorch, using a sweeping motion for even cooking. If you're using a grill, cook the shrimp over a high flame for 30 seconds to 1 minute. Remember, you want to char the outside but not overcook the shrimp.

Serve with a drizzle of olive oil, lemon wedges, and some additional red pepper flakes if you like it hot.

While scampi is technically a pasta dish, we all know that it's one of the best showcases for delicious shrimp! That's why the recipe you find here is all about respecting the star ingredient. The white wine sauce combines the traditional Italian flavors of garlic, white wine, and olive oil—flavors that are strong, but not too strong. With ample parsley, this dish is light and fresh, and with just a small hit of chile pepper flakes, lively as well.

SHRIMP SCAMPI

⊹ 135°F/57°C | ⏲ 15 MINUTES | ✗ SERVES 4

INGREDIENTS

5 tablespoons/75 ml olive oil

4 garlic cloves, minced

½ cup/120 ml white wine

1½ pounds/680 g small to medium-size shrimp, peeled and deveined, tail on

12 ounces/340 g spaghetti

½ cup/25 g chopped fresh parsley

1 to 2 teaspoons/1.8 to 3.6 g red pepper flakes, to taste

2 tablespoons/28 g unsalted butter, melted

Sea salt and black pepper

DIRECTIONS

Preheat a sous vide water bath to 135°F/57°C.

Meanwhile, heat the olive oil in a large pot over medium heat. Fry the garlic in the oil for a few minutes until fragrant. Turn the heat up to high and pour in the white wine. Boil until reduced by half, 10 to 15 minutes, then decrease the heat to low while you prepare the spaghetti and shrimp.

Bring a pot of salted water to boil for the pasta. While the water heats, lay the shrimp flat in a vacuum-seal bags and seal, but don't put them in the preheated water bath just yet. When the water for the pasta is boiling, cook the spaghetti according to the package instructions. Put your shrimp in the sous vide water bath at the appropriate time. For example if your pasta takes 15 minutes, put it in straight away.

Drain the pasta in a colander, reserving some of the cooking water.

When the shrimp have finished cooking sous vide, which should be around the same time as the pasta is finished, remove them from the water bath and cut open the top of the bags. Pour any liquid from the bags into the saucepan (keeping the shrimp in the bags), along with the cooked pasta, parsley, red pepper flakes, melted butter, and salt and pepper to taste. Toss to combine, then immediately take the pot off the heat. Finally, add the shrimp. At this point, taste the pasta. If you feel that it's too dry, use some of the pasta water that you reserved; if it's just right, simply discard the pasta water.

Tearing off the sides of a crusty bread bowl to dip into a pool of creamy shrimp chowder is oh so satisfying. I like to cook the shrimp sous vide to guarantee they're perfectly tender and moist. They should be the star of the dish rather than the side show, which has been the case in some shrimp chowders I've tried.

SHRIMP CHOWDER IN A BREAD BOWL

🌡 135°F/57°C | ⏱ 15 MINUTES | 🍴 SERVES 6

INGREDIENTS

3 cups/700 ml chicken broth

2 cups/475 ml water

12 ounces/340 g small to medium-size shrimp, peeled, deveined, tails removed (reserve half of the shells)

5 tablespoons/70 g unsalted butter, divided

6 slices bacon, chopped into small strips

1 onion, julienned

6 garlic cloves, crushed

2 cups/475 ml dry white wine

1 stalk celery, sliced

4 teaspoons/16 g fresh thyme leaves, divided

2 medium potatoes, peeled and chopped into bite-size chunks

6 round bread loaves (sourdough or rye works well)

Sea salt and black pepper

1 cup/240 ml heavy cream

1 cup/240 ml milk

1 cup/100 g freshly grated Parmesan

DIRECTIONS

Preheat a sous vide water bath to 135°F/57°C.

In a saucepan, bring the chicken broth, water, and shrimp shells to a boil over high heat. Keep the mixture at a rolling boil for 10 minutes, then remove from the heat, strain, and reserve the liquid. Discard the shrimp shells.

Heat a frying pan over medium heat with 3 tablespoons of the butter and fry the bacon for a few minutes, until it begins to get crispy. Then add the onion and garlic and fry for a few minutes longer, until the onions are tender.

Add the white wine, celery, 2 teaspoons of the thyme leaves, the potatoes, and the stock that you prepared. Keep at a rolling boil for 10 to 15 minutes, or until the potatoes are soft, pushing the potatoes around every few minutes to mash them slightly to thicken the soup.

While the soup boils, prepare the bread and shrimp. First, chop off the top of the round loaves with a bread knife and hollow out the middle with your hands; you can discard the middle or save it to use as bread crumbs in another dish. Next, lay the shrimp flat in vacuum-seal bags with the remaining 2 tablespoons butter and salt and black pepper to taste, and seal.

After the soup has been boiling for 10 to 15 minutes (when the potatoes are soft), spend a couple of minutes mashing some of the potatoes with a spatula until about half of them are mashed and the soup has thickened. Decrease the heat to low to maintain a simmer and stir in the cream and milk. Simmer for 15 minutes to allow the flavors to develop—if it gets too thick, you can add some water.

Meanwhile, put the bag of sealed shrimp into the preheated water bath and cook for 15 minutes. Cut open the vacuum-seal bags and tip the liquid from the bags into the soup (keeping the shrimp in the bags). Stir the Parmesan into the soup. Generously season with salt and black pepper, tasting until you get it just right.

Ladle the soup into the bread bowls that you hollowed out earlier. Place a few shrimp on top of each soup. Garnish with some more black pepper and the remaining 2 teaspoons thyme leaves.

A good lobster roll combines convenient food with a bit of indulgence. I've found that lobster tails cook best at a different temperature and time than the claws. Since it's lobster, it seems worth the extra effort to me! If you can get hold of New England–style split-top hot dog buns, that's what you'll want to use here. If not, regular hot dog buns sliced horizontally will work just fine.

LOBSTER ROLL WITH WARM LEMON BUTTER

♨ 133°F/56°C (TAILS), 140°F/60°C (CLAWS)

🕐 15 MINUTES (TAILS), 15 MINUTES (CLAWS) | ✗ SERVES 4

INGREDIENTS

4 medium lobsters (around 1½ pounds/680 g each)

4 New England–style split-top hot dog buns or regular hot dog buns

1 lemon, sliced into wedges

LEMON BUTTER DRESSING

¼ cup/56 g unsalted butter, melted and still warm

¼ cup/60 ml freshly squeezed lemon juice

2 tablespoons/5 g finely chopped fresh chives, plus extra to garnish

1 tablespoon/8 g drained capers, chopped

Salt and black pepper

Pinch of cayenne (optional)

DIRECTIONS

Bring a large pot of water to a boil. Submerge the lobsters in the boiling water and immediately remove the pot from the heat. Leave the lobsters in the water for 2 minutes, then remove them and immediately plunge them in an ice bath for 5 to 10 minutes. With scissors, carefully remove the lobster shells.

Preheat a sous vide water bath to 133°F/56°C.

Seal the peeled lobster tails in individual vacuum-seal bags and cook in the preheated water bath for 15 minutes. When the lobster has finished cooking, remove the bags and plunge them into an ice-water bath (this is to shock the temperature and stop them from cooking; you will warm them again slightly before serving).

Raise the temperature of the water bath to 140°F/60°C. Seal the lobster claws in vacuum-seal bags and cook in the preheated water bath for 15 minutes.

While the lobster claws cook, make the dressing by mixing all of the dressing ingredients together in a medium-size bowl.

When the claws have 3 minutes left of sous vide cooking time, add the tails back into the bath to warm. When the claws are cooked, remove all the bags from the water bath and set aside on the counter.

Remove all of the lobster from the bags, discarding any liquid. Slice the lobster tails lengthwise into 2 to 4 strips, depending on how chunky you want your lobster pieces. Add all the lobster to the dressing bowl and gently coat in the warm lemon butter dressing.

Heat a grill or frying pan over medium heat and toast the sliced buns. Fill the warm toasted buns with the dressed lobster pieces. Garnish with extra chives, salt and black pepper, and cayenne (if you'd like). Serve with lemon wedges.

In Bermuda, the fish sandwich is something of an obsession. Either deep fried or simply grilled, fish sandwiches are often served with coleslaw (which is sometimes spicy) and tartar sauce. When I spent time there on vacation, I found each bar and restaurant has its own take on this island staple, varying the fish, bread, and trimmings. I go extra tropical with a charred slice of pineapple. Although this may seem strange if you haven't tried a fish sandwich with pineapple in it before, it's a natural fit—even more so than Hawaiian pizza! The fish and pineapple are complemented here with a hit of spicy mayo.

SEASIDE FISH SANDWICH WITH CHARRED PINEAPPLE

🌡 131°F/55°C | 🕐 30 MINUTES (SEE NOTE) | 🍴 SERVES 4

Note: The timing in this recipe is based on a fish fillet that's 1 to 1½ inches/3 to 4 cm thick. If you have a much thinner piece of fish, decrease the cooking time to 20 minutes.

INGREDIENTS

2 (6- to 7-ounce/170- to 200-g) skinless white fish fillets (such as mahi mahi, tilapia, or cod), 1 to 1½ inches/3 to 4 cm thick, cut in half (to make 4 pieces of fish)

1 lemon, divided

2 tablespoons/30 ml olive oil

4 pineapple rings

Salt and pepper

2 tablespoons/30 ml vegetable oil

Butter lettuce leaves

4 soft burger buns (soft and slightly sweet buns work best here)

4 slices tomato

GARLIC AND CHILE MAYO

¼ cup/56 g whole-egg mayonnaise

4 teaspoons/20 ml fresh lemon juice

2 garlic cloves, crushed

4 teaspoons/20 ml hot sauce

DIRECTIONS

Preheat a sous vide water bath to 131°F/55°C.

Place 2 fish halves (1 whole fillet) in each of 2 vacuum-seal bags. Cut the lemon in half. Cut one half of the lemon into 4 thin slices and add 2 slices to each bag (reserve the other lemon half to squeeze on the fish later). Add 1 tablespoon of the olive oil to each bag and seal the bags. Cook in the preheated water bath for 30 minutes.

To make the mayo, combine all the ingredients in a small bowl, cover, and refrigerate.

When the fish has about 5 minutes of cooking time left on it, heat a grill pan over high heat. Pat the pineapple slices dry with paper towels and fry for 1 to 2 minutes on each side, or until you get some grill lines (a blowtorch will help you get some char faster; if you go this route, give the pineapple a torch while in the pan and decrease the cooking time slightly). Set the pineapple slices aside on a chopping board.

Turn the heat to high and let the grill pan get very hot. While the pan heats, remove the fish from the water bath, cut the bags open, and pat the fish dry. Season the fish with salt and pepper, add vegetable oil, and then sear in the hot pan for 10 to 30 seconds on each side (you don't want the fish to overcook!). I recommend only frying 1 or 2 pieces of fish at a time. And again, if you have a blowtorch, you can use it here (torching also helps impart some smoky flavor without overcooking the fish). As soon as you have some color on the fish, carefully remove from the pan, set on a clean plate or cutting board, and squeeze some juice from the remaining lemon half over the top.

Assemble the sandwiches with lettuce on the bottom half of the burger bun, followed by a slice of tomato, then the fish, then a pineapple ring. Generously smear some mayo on each bun top and place that on the pineapple ring.

The perfect fish taco is all about balance: creamy guacamole, acidity from salsa and lime juice, and soft fish all wrapped up in a warm tortilla. The fish is the star of the show, though, so getting it right is key. This recipe calls for you to poach the fish fillets in milk and then shred them into tender, bite-size pieces. By cooking the fish sous vide, and then not searing it to finish, no moisture is lost, so its texture is super-soft and silky.

You can make this recipe as simple or as hands-on as you want it to be, as you can always opt for store-bought salsa, guac, and/or tortillas, but I really do recommend making them all yourself because they're worlds apart from the store-bought stuff!

FISH TACOS WITH CHUNKY SALSA, AVOCADO SMASH, AND CHARRED LIME

🌡 131°F/55°C | 🕐 30 MINUTES (SEE NOTE) | ✕ SERVES 4

Note: The timing in this recipe is based on a fish fillet that's 1 to 1½ inches/3 to 4 cm thick. If you have a much thinner piece of fish, decrease the cooking time to 20 minutes.

INGREDIENTS

CHUNKY SALSA

8 Roma tomatoes, diced

4 garlic cloves, diced

½ red onion, diced

2 scallions, diced

2 tablespoons/8 g chopped fresh cilantro

1 tablespoon/15 ml olive oil

Juice of 1 lime

Salt and black pepper to taste

1 tablespoon/8 g diced jalapeño

Chili powder to taste (optional)

FISH

2 (6- to 7-ounce/170- to 200-g) skinless white fish fillets (such as mahi mahi, tilapia, or cod), 1 to 1½ inches/3 to 4 cm thick

Salt and pepper

¼ cup/60 ml whole milk

Juice of 1 lime

HOMEMADE FLOUR TORTILLAS (MAKES 8)

2 cups/240 g all-purpose flour

½ teaspoon/3 g salt

¾ cup/180 ml water

3 tablespoons/45 ml olive oil

½ cup/120 ml vegetable oil, for frying (optional)

AVOCADO SMASH

2 ripe avocados, peeled, pitted, and roughly mashed with a fork

½ cup/56 g crumbled feta

1 tablespoon/ 6¼ g chopped fresh cilantro

Squeeze of fresh lime juice

Sea salt to taste

4 limes, to serve

DIRECTIONS

To make the salsa, 12 hours or the night before you want to eat the fish tacos, mix all of the salsa ingredients together in a medium-size bowl. Cover and refrigerate.

When you're ready to start the tacos, give yourself about an hour. The goal is to start the fish and then make the avocado smash and the tortillas while the fish cooks.

Preheat a sous vide water bath to 131°F/55°C.

To prepare the fish, season the fish fillets with salt and pepper. Place in individual resealable plastic bags along with 2 tablespoons of milk in each bag. Seal using the displacement method (see page 14), clip the bags to the side of the preheated water bath, and cook for 30 minutes.

To make the tortillas, combine the flour and salt in a large bowl, then mix in the water and olive oil. Knead the mixture on a lightly floured surface for a minute, or until smooth. Return the dough to the bowl, cover, and let rest for 10 minutes.

While the dough rests, prepare the avocado smash by combining all of the ingredients in a medium-size bowl and mashing them with a fork until roughly combined.

After the dough has rested for 10 minutes, divide it into 8 portions and roll each portion into a circle 7 to 9 inches/18 to 23 cm wide. Heat a nonstick pan over medium heat and add 1 tablespoon of the vegetable oil (or the garlic oil on page 270). Or, if you want soft, floury tortillas, don't use any oil (and make sure your pan is nonstick!).

Fry 1 tortilla at a time for about 1 minute on each side, or until lightly browned. Transfer to a plate and cover with foil. Repeat with the remaining dough, adding 1 tablespoon of the vegetable oil each time (if using). If you're making crispy tacos and want them to be that "taco" shape, form them into the shape that you want straight out of the pan. Use tongs to drape them over something such as the rungs of an oven rack and allow them to cool in that position. Once they begin to cool they'll hold whatever shape they're in.

Once you're done with the tortillas, cut the cheeks off 4 limes, discarding the center, and char the lime pieces quickly in a pan over high heat.

When the fish has finished cooking sous vide, drain the excess liquid from the bags and then tip the contents into a medium-size bowl. Squeeze the juice of 1 lime over the fish and shred it into bite-size chunks. Serve with the avocado smash, chunky salsa, tortillas, and charred lime cheeks.

The texture of this tuna is simply divine. I've found both salmon and tuna benefit from a brine, which boosts the flavor and moisture. After 6 hours in the fridge, the cool tuna slices are smooth and slightly firm, yet the tuna is still a vibrant red. Here I've served it with an olive tapenade, basil leaves, a drizzle of olive oil, and some lemon wedges. This recipe may seem like a bit of an ordeal at first glance, since it does take just over 7 hours, but it can be done overnight if you prefer.

RARE TUNA WITH OLIVE TAPENADE

🌡 104°F/40°C | 🕐 1 HOUR | 🍴 SERVES 4

INGREDIENTS

BRINE

3 cups/700 ml water

2 cups/280 g ice

½ cup/124 g kosher salt

¼ cup/50 g sugar

TUNA

2 tuna steaks (6 to 7 ounces/170 to 200 g each)

¼ cup/60 ml olive oil, plus extra to serve

1 cup/30 g baby spinach leaves

2 tablespoons/12 g small to medium-size fresh basil leaves, to garnish

Flaky sea salt

1 lemon, cut into 8 wedges

OLIVE TAPENADE

¼ cup/60 ml olive oil

1 cup/100 g pitted black olives

2 tablespoons/12 g fresh basil leaves, plus more small leaves, to serve

1 tablespoon/8 g drained capers

4 anchovies

1 tablespoon/15 ml freshly squeezed lemon juice

1 garlic clove, roughly chopped

Salt and black pepper to taste

DIRECTIONS

To make the brine, combine the ingredients in a large bowl and whisk until the salt and sugar have dissolved.

To make the tuna, add the tuna steaks to the brine, cover, and refrigerate for about 45 minutes, stirring the water and flipping the tuna every 10 to 15 minutes to ensure even brining.

With about 20 minutes left on the brine, preheat a sous vide water bath to 104°F/40°C.

After 45 minutes in the brine, take the tuna steaks out of the brine and pat them dry. Transfer the tuna to individual vacuum-seal bags with 2 tablespoons of olive oil in each. Seal and cook in the preheated water bath for 1 hour. Transfer the bags to an ice water bath for 5 to 10 minutes. Once the tuna steaks are cool, refrigerate them (still in the vacuum-seal bags) for 6 hours or overnight. This step is important to set the tuna.

At some point while the tuna is chilling, make the olive tapenade. Combine all of the olive tapenade ingredients in a food processor and process until the mixture forms a chunky paste. Transfer the olive tapenade to a small bowl, cover, and refrigerate.

Once the tuna steaks have been in the fridge for at least 6 hours or overnight, they're ready to serve. Divide the spinach among 4 plates. Slice the steaks into strips and arrange them on top of the spinach. Spoon tapenade over the tuna slices and arrange the basil leaves on top. Drizzle extra olive oil over the tuna and salad, and scatter some flaky sea salt over the top. Serve with lemon wedges.

The process of brining, cooking sous vide, and then chilling to set the salmon results in a silky, slightly firm texture that any salmon lover will revel in. Just like the tuna on page 159, salmon gets a flavor and moisture boost after just 45 minutes in a brine! This recipe may seem like a bit of an ordeal at first glance, since it does take just over 7 hours, but it can be done overnight if you prefer. However, most of that time is hands-off, and when you try this salmon along with the creamy, zesty dill crème fraîche, I guarantee you'll think the time spent was worthwhile.

SILKY SALMON WITH DILL CRÈME FRAÎCHE

⧉* 122°F/50°C | 🕐 20 MINUTES | 🍴 SERVES 4

INGREDIENTS

BRINE

3 cups/700 ml water

2 cups/280 g ice

½ cup/124 g kosher salt

¼ cup/25 g sugar

SALMON

2 skinless salmon fillets (6 to 7 ounces/170 to 200 g each), deboned

½ cup/120 ml olive oil (or a mixture of ¼ cup/60 ml olive oil, ¼ cup/60 ml canola oil)

1 tablespoon/8 g drained capers

¼ cup/10 g thinly sliced fresh chives

1 lemon, cut into 8 wedges

DILL CRÈME FRAÎCHE

7 ounces/200 g crème fraîche

2 tablespoons/6 g finely chopped fresh dill

1 tablespoon/15 g Dijon mustard

1 tablespoon/15 ml white wine vinegar

2 teaspoons/10 ml freshly squeezed lemon juice

Sea salt and black pepper to taste

DIRECTIONS

To make the brine, combine all the ingredients in a large bowl and whisk until the salt and sugar have dissolved, around 1 to 2 minutes.

To prepare the salmon, add the salmon fillets to the brine, cover, and refrigerate for 45 minutes, stirring the water and flipping the salmon halfway through to ensure even brining.

With about 20 minutes left on the brine, preheat a sous vide water bath to 122°F/50°C.

When the brining time is up, take the salmon fillets out of the brine and pat them dry. Transfer them to individual resealable plastic bags with ¼ cup/60 ml of oil in each bag. Seal using the displacement method (see page 14), clip the bag to the side of the preheated water bath, and cook for 20 minutes. Transfer the bags to an ice water bath for 5 to 10 minutes. Once cool, refrigerate the salmon (still in the bags) for 6 hours or overnight. This step is important to set the salmon.

While the salmon is in the fridge (or at some point during cooking), make the dill crème fraîche. Whisk together the ingredients in a medium-size bowl, cover, and refrigerate until it's time to serve the salmon.

Once the salmon has been in the fridge for at least 6 hours or overnight, it's ready to serve. Now it's time to get artistic! Cut the fillets into bite-size pieces and arrange them on a plate. Pipe or spoon the dill crème fraîche onto the plate. Arrange the capers on the plate, scatter the sliced chives over the top, and serve with lemon wedges.

This recipe hits perfectly pink salmon with the crunchy texture and unique flavors of a dukkah-inspired topping. Chopped nuts, ample herbs, and yogurt tahini enhance the Middle Eastern flavors. If you have the time, brining the salmon first helps it retain moisture and gives it a silkier texture. If not, don't fret; it's still fantastic without brining.

SALMON FILLET WITH HERBED TAHINI

🌡* 122°F/50°C | 🕐 20 MINUTES | 🍴 SERVES 4

INGREDIENTS

BRINE

3 cups/700 ml water

2 cups/280 g ice

½ cup/124 g kosher salt

¼ cup/25 g sugar

SALMON

4 skinless salmon fillets (3½ ounces/100 g each), deboned

½ cup/120 ml olive oil (or ¼ cup/60 ml olive oil, ¼ cup/60 ml canola oil)

Salt and pepper

TAHINI YOGURT

1 cup/227 g plain yogurt

3 tablespoons/45 g tahini

1 garlic clove, minced

2 teaspoons/10 ml freshly squeezed lemon juice

Salt and black pepper

HERBY DUKKAH

2 tablespoons/6 g finely chopped fresh parsley

2 tablespoons/6 g finely chopped fresh mint

1 shallot, finely chopped

½ tablespoon/4 g toasted, finely chopped hazelnuts

½ tablespoon/4 g toasted, finely chopped almonds

½ teaspoon/1½ g lemon zest

Salt and black pepper

DIRECTIONS

To make the brine, combine the ingredients in a large bowl and whisk until the salt and sugar have dissolved, around 1 to 2 minutes.

To prepare the salmon, add the salmon fillets to the brine, cover, and refrigerate for 45 minutes, stirring the water and flipping the salmon halfway through to ensure even brining.

With about 20 minutes left on the brine, preheat a sous vide water bath to 122°F/50°C.

When the salmon has finished brining, remove it from the brine and rinse with cold water. Season the salmon with salt and pepper and place it in a resealable plastic bag with the olive oil. Seal using the displacement method (see page 14), clip the bag to the side of the preheated water bath, and cook for 20 minutes.

Meanwhile, to make the tahini yoghurt, mix together the ingredients in a small bowl.

To make the herby dukkah, in a separate small bowl, combine the ingredients and mix well.

When the salmon is finished cooking, carefully remove the fillets from the bag and plate the salmon. (You can discard any cooking liquid.) Smear a large spoonful of the tahini yogurt on top of the salmon fillets, then dust the herby dukkah on top of the yogurt.

This recipe is your secret to foolproof, tender octopus. I've found this caper butter drizzle really brings out the best in octopus, but by all means try serving it another way as well. In keeping with the Mediterranean theme, I've also created a chickpea purée to serve alongside this dish. Hopefully, it will help you imagine you're in a little café down a cobblestoned street on the coast of Santorini!

OIL-POACHED OCTOPUS WITH CAPER BUTTER

🌡 171°F/77°C | ⏱ 7 HOURS | 🍴 SERVES 4

INGREDIENTS

OCTOPUS

8 fresh or frozen octopus legs (around 1½ pounds/680 g), thawed if frozen

2 cups/475 ml olive oil

Sea salt and black pepper

Lemon wedges (optional)

Chopped fresh parsley (optional)

CHICKPEA PURÉE

1 cup/240 ml olive oil or vegetable oil

4 cups/655 g cooked chickpeas

8 garlic cloves, minced

2 cups/475 ml water

Dash of cayenne pepper, to taste

Sea salt and black pepper

CAPER BUTTER DRIZZLE

4 heaping teaspoons/about 35 g drained capers

1½ tablespoons/22 ½ g sherry vinegar or red wine vinegar

3 tablespoons/42 g unsalted butter

Sea salt and black pepper

DIRECTIONS

Preheat a sous vide water bath to 171°F/77°C.

To prepare the octopus, place the tentacles into resalable plastic bags, 2 per bag, and pour ½ cup/120 ml of the olive oil into each bag. Seal using the displacement method (see page 14), clip the bag to the side of the preheated water bath, and cook for 7 hours.

With 30 minutes left on the octopus, make the chickpea purée. Set a saucepan over medium-low heat, add 1 cup/240 ml olive oil, and cook the chickpeas and garlic for 5 minutes, or until the chickpeas start to darken. Add 2 cups/475 ml of the water and bring the mixture to a boil over high heat, then decrease the heat to medium and simmer for 10 minutes, or until most of the water has been absorbed.

Meanwhile, to make the caper butter drizzle, heat a small saucepan over medium heat. Add all the ingredients and stir well to combine. Cook for about 5 minutes to melt the butter and combine the flavors. Squash the capers down with a spatula a bit as well. Decrease the heat to very low and keep the mixture warm until you're ready to serve.

After the chickpea liquid has finished reducing, transfer to a blender and purée. Season with cayenne pepper, sea salt, and black pepper to taste. Remove the bags the octopus was cooked in from the sous vide water bath, pour the liquid into a measuring cup and measure ½ cup/120 ml total. Add it to the blender and then give the mixture another blitz to combine.

Transfer the caper butter to a medium bowl. Using tongs, transfer the octopus from the resealable bags into the dressing bowl, leaving any remaining olive oil in the bags. Generously cover the octopus with the dressing.

Spoon the chickpea purée onto each of 4 serving dishes, top each with 2 octopus tentacles, and then spoon over some additional caper butter. Serve with lemon wedges and chopped parsley, or garnish as you'd like.

Calamari is notoriously easy to overcook. Although it is delicious when tender, when overcooked it takes on an unpleasant rubber band–like texture. And nobody wants that. Cooking the calamari sous vide before battering and frying helps break down that toughness, meaning you're left with foolproof rings that are ready for a quick flash in the deep fryer to crisp them up. It might not be the traditional Spanish way, but it definitely helps you get tender calamari every time. (If battered seafood isn't your thing, check out the recipe for Oil-Poached Octopus with Caper Butter on page 167.)

CRISPY CALAMARI

🌡 136°F/58°C | 🕐 1½ HOURS | 🍴 SERVES 4

INGREDIENTS

1 to 1½ pounds/450 to 680 g fresh or frozen calamari rings (defrosted, if frozen)

1 cup/120 g tempura batter mix

1 cup/240 ml soda water

Vegetable oil, for deep frying

Salt and black pepper to taste

Shredded lettuce, to serve

Lemon wedges, to serve

DIRECTIONS

Preheat a sous vide water bath to 136°F/58°C.

Seal the calamari rings flat in vacuum-seal bags and cook in the preheated water bath for 1½ hours. When the calamari rings are done, cut open the bag and discard any liquid.

Add the tempura batter to a medium-size mixing bowl, then stir the soda water into the batter until you get a consistency that thinly coats your finger when you dip it in. Pour at least 4 inches/10 cm of vegetable oil into a deep fryer or pot and heat to 375°F/191°C.

Working in batches, dip the calamari rings into the batter, then into the hot oil and fry for 3 to 4 minutes, or until the batter is browned.

Transfer the cooked calamari to paper towels and season with salt and pepper. Serve on shredded lettuce with lemon wedges, or however you prefer.

CHAPTER 6
A TRIP THROUGH ASIA

Pork Buns

Char Siu Chinese Barbecue Pork Loin

Hong Kong–Style Flat Noodles with
Sliced Beef

Crispy Duck Pancakes with Hoisin Sauce

Butter Chicken with Cashews

Lamb Rogan Josh

Penang Curry Chicken

Red Curry with Sliced Duck Breast

Coconut-Poached Cod in Tom Kha Broth

Shrimp Summer Rolls

Shredded Chicken Bánh Mì

Miso-Marinated Black Cod

Duck Gyoza

Ramen with Sticky Pork Belly

This recipe takes tender sous vide pork belly and gives it an Asian twist. When you coat the sous vide belly slices in hoisin and sear them under the broiler for a few minutes, the result is tender pork with a little bit of char on the outside. Wrapping them in steamed buns makes for a great snack or light meal that even those hesitant to try exotic foods will absolutely love.

PORK BUNS

🌡 158°F/70°C | 🕐 24 HOURS | 🍴 SERVES 6

INGREDIENTS

2 pounds/900 g pork belly, excess fat from the top layer trimmed

18 frozen or fresh Chinese steamed buns

1 cup/240 ml hoisin sauce, plus a few tablespoons extra to serve

1 cup/240 ml Sweet 'n' Sticky Barbecue Sauce (at right) or your favorite sauce

Handful of scallions, julienned

1 cucumber, julienned

1 large red fresh chile pepper, sliced

2 tablespoons/8 g cilantro leaves

SWEET 'N' STICKY BARBECUE SAUCE

1 tablespoon/14 g butter

1 tablespoon/15 ml vegetable oil

2 tablespoons/20 g finely diced onion

6 garlic cloves, finely diced

¼ cup/53 g brown sugar

3 tablespoons/45 ml apple cider vinegar

2 tablespoons/30 ml water

1 tablespoon/15 g paprika

1¼ cups/300 g ketchup

¾ cup/170 g tomato paste

1 tablespoon/15 ml Worcestershire sauce

1 teaspoon/6 g salt

1 teaspoon/2½ g black pepper

DIRECTIONS

Preheat a sous vide water bath to 158°F/70°C.

Seal the pork belly in vacuum-seal bags. Depending on the size of your bags, you may need to slice the belly in half. Cook in the preheated water bath for 24 hours.

While the pork belly is cooking, make the barbecue sauce. Melt the butter in a saucepan over medium heat. Once it's melted, add the vegetable oil and fry the onion and garlic for a few minutes, until the onion softens and the butter browns. Add the brown sugar and vinegar and decrease the heat to low. Cook for 15 minutes, adding the water after about 5 minutes, or when the sauce gets very sticky. Stir every few minutes and scrape up any bits from the bottom of the pot. After 15 minutes of caramelizing, add the paprika, chili powder, ketchup, tomato paste, Worcestershire sauce, salt, and pepper, scraping any garlic and onion off the bottom with a spatula. Bring to a boil over high heat, then decrease the heat and simmer for 20 minutes, or until the flavors develop and the sauce thickens. Transfer to a storage container and refrigerate until the next day.

The next day, at the 24-hour mark, preheat your broiler to the highest setting (you can leave the pork in the sous vide water bath as you do these next steps).

Steam the buns for the specified time on the package. Once they're cooked, slice them down the middle for stuffing.

When the pork has finished cooking sous vide, mix together the hoisin and 1 cup/240 ml of barbecue sauce. Take the pork out of the vacuum-seal bags, slice thinly, and coat well with the sauce mixture. Lay out the pork slices on a baking tray covered in parchment or foil, and put under the preheated broiler for a few minutes—just until you get some good color on the surface.

To assemble the buns, fill the Chinese steamed buns with the pork, a drizzle of hoisin, and the scallions, cucumber, chile, and cilantro.

Char siu is a street food favorite in Hong Kong (my adopted home growing up as a British expat). Wandering down the streets you'll see bright red sticky pork loins as well as whole glazed roasted ducks hanging in countless shop windows. At home, though, char siu is often seen as too time-consuming. That's where sous vide comes in. I've devised a recipe that takes the laborious element out of the prep and also guarantees tender pork every time—something that you don't always get with the classic street food versions. I've found it goes equally well with rice and scallions, steamed Chinese vegetables, fried noodles, noodle soup, and ramen (page 206).

CHAR SIU CHINESE BARBECUE PORK LOIN

♨ 136°F/58°C | 🕐 2 HOURS | ✗ SERVES 4

INGREDIENTS

CHAR SIU MARINADE

½ cup/120 ml hoisin sauce

½ cup/120 ml honey

2 tablespoons rice vinegar/30 ml (or apple cider vinegar if you can't find rice vinegar)

2 tablespoons/30 ml light soy sauce

1 tablespoon peanut oil/30 ml or vegetable oil

1 teaspoon/5 g five-spice powder

1 teaspoon/5 ml red food coloring (optional)

1 pound/450 g pork tenderloin

GLAZE

3 tablespoons/45 ml hoisin sauce

2 tablespoons/30 ml honey

2 teaspoons/12 g salt, or to taste

DIRECTIONS

To make the marinade, combine all of the ingredients in a bowl and stir to blend, then pour into a resealable plastic bag. Add the pork, seal, and refrigerate overnight.

The next day, preheat a sous vide water bath to 136°F/58°C.

Remove the pork from the resealable plastic bag, discarding the excess marinade, and seal the pork in a vacuum-seal bag. Cook in the preheated water bath for 2 hours.

To make the glaze, combine the glaze ingredients in a small bowl.

When the pork has around 5 minutes left of sous vide cooking, prepare for the finishing step. A blowtorch is ideal, but if you don't have one, a broiler on the highest setting will do.

When the pork has finished cooking sous vide, brush the glaze onto the pork. Torch the outside of the pork (see pages 33 to 35) or place it on a baking sheet under the preheated broiler on the highest setting, just until you get some good color on the outside (you don't want the meat to dry out, which is surprisingly easy!). Thinly slice the pork with a sharp knife and serve with the extra glaze as a sauce/dipping sauce.

In addition to the tasty flavor, this dish has a lot of fun textures—tender beef, crunchy bean sprouts, and chewy flat rice noodles. Just be careful when cooking the rice noodles: they're very easy to overcook, so you don't want to leave them in the wok for too long. The secret to the perfect texture and flavor of chow fun noodles is using a very hot cooking temperature for a fast cooking time and a kiss of smoke from the wok. If done right, this is a fast dish that takes just a minute or so of actual wok time, so make sure all of your ingredients are prepped and ready to go beforehand.

HONG KONG-STYLE FLAT NOODLES WITH SLICED BEEF

🌡 129°F/54°C | ⏱ 2 HOURS | 🍴 SERVES 4

INGREDIENTS

12 ounces/340 g flank steak

STIR-FRY SAUCE

1 tablespoon/30 ml hoisin sauce

1 tablespoon/15 ml light soy sauce

1 tablespoon/30 ml oyster sauce

2 teaspoons/10 ml dark soy sauce

2 teaspoons/10 ml Shaoxing wine or rice vinegar

NOODLES AND VEGETABLES

2 pounds/900 g fresh flat, wide rice noodles

Salt and white pepper to taste

3 tablespoons/30 ml vegetable oil, divided

1 white onion, julienned

2 tablespoons/12 g thinly sliced ginger

8 scallions, trimmed, split in half vertically, and cut into 3-inch/7 cm pieces

2 cups/200 g fresh bean sprouts

Chopped small fresh red chiles (optional, to garnish)

DIRECTIONS

Preheat a sous vide water bath to 129°F/54°C.

Seal the steak in a vacuum-seal bag and cook in the preheated water bath for 2 hours.

Meanwhile, to make the sauce, combine all the sauce ingredients in a medium-size bowl and set aside.

To make the noodles and vegetables, when the steak has finished cooking sous vide, soak the rice noodles according to the package directions. If your noodles don't have any instructions for presoaking, then place the noodles in a large bowl and pour some boiling water over to help them separate. Leave the noodles in the hot water for approximately 3 minutes, loosening them with tongs or chopsticks every so often. Drain and set aside.

Remove the steak from the bag and pat dry. Season it generously with salt and pepper. Heat a work or large skillet over high heat until it just starts to smoke, then add 1 tablespoon of the vegetable oil and fry the steak for 1 minute on each side. Remove from the heat, transfer the steak to a chopping board, and slice as thinly as you can.

Place the wok or large frying pan over high heat until smoking hot. Add the remaining 2 tablespoons vegetable oil. Within a 30-second to 1-minute time frame, add the onion, ginger, and scallions and fry for a few seconds, then add the rice noodles, followed by the stir-fry sauce, and finally the bean sprouts, tossing the ingredients the whole time to combine (but be careful not to break the noodles!). Stir-fry for about 30 more seconds once all of the ingredients are in the wok, continuing to toss. The whole process should take 1 to 1½ minutes. Take the wok or skillet off the heat and add the beef.

Serve immediately. To spice it up, top with some chopped fresh chiles.

Using conventional cooking methods at home, this take-out favorite hardly ever turns out like you want it to—either because the duck meat is overcooked or because the skin just doesn't crisp up properly. My goal with this recipe was to get the duck as tender as possible using sous vide, and then crisp it up with a flash fry in a deep fryer right at the end. Why choose either crispy but dry or moist but with no crust when you can have it all?

CRISPY DUCK PANCAKES WITH HOISIN SAUCE

🌡 167°F/75°C | ⏱ 10 HOURS | 🍴 SERVES 4

INGREDIENTS

4 skin-on duck legs

15 Chinese-style pancakes or small flour tortillas, to serve

Vegetable oil, for deep frying

Salt

½ cup/120 ml hoisin sauce

1 cup/64 g julienned scallion

1 cup/120 g julienned cucumber

DIRECTIONS

Preheat a sous vide water bath to 167°F/75°C.

Seal the duck legs in vacuum-seal bags, around 2 per bag, and cook in the preheated water bath for 10 hours.

When you are almost ready to serve, heat the Chinese-style pancakes according to the package directions.

Pour at least 4 inches/10 cm of vegetable oil into a deep fryer or pot and heat to 400°F/200°C. While the oil heats, remove the duck from the bags and pat dry. Season the legs with salt and deep-fry them in the hot oil for 1 to 2 minutes, or until the skin becomes crispy.

Serve with the hoisin sauce, the julienned scallion and cucumber, and the warmed Chinese-style pancakes.

Are you ready for butter chicken where the chicken can be cut with a butter knife? Look no further: you'll find juicy, perfectly cooked chicken in this rich curry. If you're unfamiliar with the dish, butter chicken (murgh makhani) can be a weeknight family meal or it can be the perfect hangover cure! It's a belly-warming dish, but unlike some Indian dishes, it's not too spicy, so those who are sensitive to chile can still dig in.

BUTTER CHICKEN WITH CASHEWS

🌡 150°F/66°C | ⏱ 2 HOURS | 🍴 SERVES 4

INGREDIENTS

8 boneless, skinless chicken thighs

¼ cup/30 g cashews

3 tablespoons/42 g unsalted butter

6 cardamom pods

4 cloves

1 tablespoon/5 ml cumin seeds, ground

2 star anise

6 garlic cloves, crushed

1-inch/2 cm piece ginger, peeled and sliced

1 onion, julienned

1 teaspoon/5 ml fenugreek seeds, ground (optional; okay to omit if you can't find them)

3 cups/700 ml tomato sauce

2 bay leaves

1 cinnamon stick

1 tablespoon/9 g garam masala

1 tablespoon/15 g paprika

1 teaspoon turmeric

Salt and black pepper to taste

1 teaspoon to 1 tablespoon/5 to 15 g chili powder, to taste

1¼ cups/300 ml heavy cream

Rice, to serve

Naan bread or chapatis, to serve

¼ cup/20 g sliced almonds, toasted (optional, to garnish)

¼ cup/12 g roughly torn cilantro (optional, to garnish)

DIRECTIONS

Preheat a sous vide water bath to 150°F/66°C.

Seal the chicken thighs in vacuum-seal bags and cook in the preheated water bath for 2 hours.

Using a blender, blend the cashews with 1 cup/240 ml of water until puréed and set aside.

Heat a medium-size pot over medium-high heat. When it's nice and hot, melt the butter in the pot and fry the cardamom pods and cloves for a couple of minutes, or until fragrant. Add the cumin seeds, star anise, garlic, ginger, onion, and ground fenugreek. Fry, stirring, for about 10 minutes, or until the onions begin to caramelize. Add the tomato sauce, bay leaves, cinnamon stick, garam masala, paprika, turmeric, salt and pepper to taste, and chili powder, then bring the sauce to a boil. Add the cashew nut and water mixture to the curry, then decrease the heat to low. Cover and simmer the curry very gently over low heat until the chicken has almost finished cooking (make sure it's not bubbling, or else too much sauce will evaporate).

When the chicken has around 10 minutes of sous vide cooking left, strain the curry through a wire strainer, discarding the solids. Pour the liquid curry back into the pot. Stir in the cream, let it warm through, then remove the pot from the heat. If the curry has become too thick, you can add a little water.

When the chicken has finished cooking sous vide, take it out of the vacuum-seal bags and chop it into bite-size chunks. Stir the chicken chunks into the curry and serve with rice and naan bread or chapatis, garnished with the almonds and cilantro.

Just a quick glance at the ingredients below and you'll see that this is not a butter- and cream-laden curry. In fact, it's actually quite healthy in comparison to most curries! Yet it's so jam-packed with veggies and spices, you won't miss the fat. That's doubly true once you add sous vide lamb to the mix. Cooked for 24 hours at 140°F/60°C, this lamb is insanely tender yet still slightly pink in the middle.

LAMB ROGAN JOSH

※ 140°F/60°C | ◷ 24 HOURS | ✗ SERVES 4

INGREDIENTS

1½ to 2 pounds/680 to 900 g lamb shoulder

¼ cup/30 g cashews

¼ cup/60 ml vegetable oil

1 tablespoon/5 ml cumin seeds, ground

1 teaspoon coriander seeds, ground

1 teaspoon/5 ml fenugreek seeds, ground

1 tablespoon/15 g garam masala

2 tablespoons/30 g paprika

1 teaspoon to 1 tablespoon/5 to 15 g chili powder, to taste

3 onions, julienned

1½ tablespoons/9 g grated ginger

1½ tablespoons/12 g crushed garlic

½ carrot, thinly sliced

2 tomatoes, roughly chopped

½ teaspoon/2½ g turmeric

2 bay leaves

¼ cup/56 g plain yogurt

Salt and pepper to taste

Chopped cilantro, to garnish

DIRECTIONS

Preheat a sous vide water bath to 140°F/60°C.

Seal the lamb shoulder in a vacuum-seal bag and cook in the preheated water bath for 24 hours.

When the lamb has around 25 minutes left of sous vide cooking time, you can begin making the sauce (you can leave the lamb in the water bath as you make the sauce even if the cooking time runs slightly over).

Using a blender, blend the cashews with 1 cup/240 ml of water until puréed and set aside.

Heat a large saucepan over medium-high heat. Add the vegetable oil and allow it to heat up, then add the cumin seeds, coriander seeds, fenugreek seeds, garam masala, paprika, and chili powder and fry for 30 seconds. Decrease the heat to low, add the onion, ginger, garlic, carrot, and tomato, and cook for 20 minutes.

When the lamb has finished cooking sous vide, cut open the vacuum-seal bag and pour all of the juices out of the bag and into the pot (you can clip the lamb that remains in the bag to the edge of the water bath to keep it warm). Stir the sauce for a few minutes, making sure to scrape up anything stuck on the bottom of the pot. Blend the sauce with a handheld immersion blender until smooth (or transfer to your blender, blend, and then return to the pot). With the pan still over low heat, add the cashew water, turmeric, and bay leaves. Simmer over low heat for 20 minutes.

Transfer the lamb to a cutting board and cut into bite-size pieces. Stir the lamb into the curry and immediately remove the pot from the heat. Stir in the yogurt slowly, one large spoonful at a time, and season the curry with salt and pepper to taste. Garnish with the cilantro.

Penang curry is creamy, slightly spicy, and packed full of fantastic Asian flavors. Despite being called "Penang" curry, this dish actually originated in Thailand and is one of the most popular dishes in the country. The base of this curry is coconut milk, which makes it nice and creamy. There are actually two different ways of making a Penang curry, one with lots of sauce (like below) and the other that is more of a dry curry. I personally prefer a lot of sauce, but if you wanted you could always reduce the sauce by two-thirds and make a drier curry.

PENANG CURRY CHICKEN

🌡 140°F/60°C | ⏱ 1¼ HOURS | ✗ SERVES 4

INGREDIENTS

4 skinless chicken breasts

Salt and pepper

2¼ cups/535 ml coconut milk, divided

2 tablespoons/30 ml vegetable oil

¼ cup/110 g Penang curry paste

2 tablespoons/30 ml fish sauce

2 tablespoons/23 g palm sugar or firmly packed light brown sugar

2 cups/100 g fresh Thai basil leaves or regular basil

4 fresh red chiles, seeded and julienned (optional, to garnish)

4 kaffir lime leaves, julienned into thin shreds (optional, to garnish)

DIRECTIONS

Preheat a sous vide water bath to 140°F/60°C.

Season the chicken breasts with salt and pepper and place 2 breasts in each of 2 vacuum-seal bags. Add 2 tablespoons of the coconut milk to each bag and seal. Cook in the preheated water bath for 1 hour 15 minutes.

When the chicken has 10 minutes left of sous vide cooking, heat the oil in a skillet over medium heat, add the Penang curry paste, and cook for 2 to 3 minutes, or until fragrant. Add the remaining 2 cups/475 ml coconut milk and simmer for about 5 minutes. Add the fish sauce, palm sugar, and Thai basil leaves, and simmer for 5 minutes more.

When the chicken has finished cooking sous vide, remove from the vacuum-seal bags, slice, and arrange in 4 bowls. Pour the Penang curry sauce over the top and garnish with the julienned chiles and kaffir lime leaves.

Red curry with duck is a classic holiday staple in Thailand, and it's one of the tougher curries to cook perfectly. Duck meat can quickly go from done to overly well done, and you'll find duck pieces peppered throughout the curry that are too dry. Admittedly, it's quite difficult to gauge and time the meat doneness when you roast it and then continue to cook it blind in a giant pot of dark curry sauce. This recipe solves that problem with sous vide, of course— the duck will even be a bit pink in the middle! Flavor-wise, you'll find this curry is rich and packed full of Thai herbs. It will be a cut above your average Thai take-out, that's for sure.

RED CURRY WITH SLICED DUCK BREAST

🌡 135°F/57°C | ⏱ 2 HOURS | 🍴 SERVES 4

INGREDIENTS

DUCK

2 skin-on duck breasts, skin scored

¼ cup/60 ml vegetable oil, divided

Sea salt

CURRY SAUCE

2 tablespoons/30 ml vegetable oil

¼ cup/110 g Thai red curry paste (or enough for a recipe of this size—some curry pastes vary dramatically in the ratio of curry to protein)

4 cups/950 ml coconut milk

¼ cup/53 g palm sugar or firmly packed light brown sugar

¼ cup/60 ml fish sauce

12 kaffir lime leaves

14 ounces/400 g chopped pineapple

7 ounces/200 g seedless grapes, halved

2 small fresh red chiles, julienned, to garnish

DIRECTIONS

Preheat a sous vide water bath to 135°F/57°C.

To make the duck, take the duck breasts out of the fridge and pat dry. Heat a skillet over high heat until smoking. Add 2 tablespoons of the vegetable oil and sear the skin-side of the duck breasts for 1 to 2 minutes. (See page 30 to learn more about pre-searing.) Seal the breasts individually in vacuum-seal bags, or 2 per bag, and cook in the preheated water bath for 2 hours.

To make the curry sauce, with 15 minutes left to go on the duck, heat the 2 tablespoons vegetable oil in a pot over medium heat and fry the Thai red curry paste for a few minutes, until fragrant. Stir in the coconut milk and bring the mixture to a boil. Decrease the heat to medium-low and add the sugar, fish sauce, and lime leaves. Simmer for 10 minutes. Add the chopped pineapple and simmer for 2 more minutes. Finally, stir in the grapes and take the pan off the heat.

When the duck has finished cooking sous vide, heat a skillet with the remaining 2 tablespoons vegetable oil over high heat. Pat the skin-side of the duck dry and season generously with salt. Fry the duck in the smoking hot skillet for 1 to 2 minutes, or until the skin is well rendered (but not too long that the meat under the surface will begin to overcook). Transfer the duck to a cutting board and slice thin. Remove the lime leaves from the curry and serve in bowls. Serve the duck on top of the curry, while the skin is still crisp. Garnish with the red chiles.

When cooked to perfection using sous vide, cod is deliciously silky. Here I've served it in a broth inspired by a Thai tom kha soup, which adds a kick of Asian flavor while still being light enough to allow you to appreciate the delicate fish.

COCONUT-POACHED COD IN TOM KHA BROTH

131°F/55°C | 30 MINUTES (SEE NOTE) | SERVES 4

Note: The timing in this recipe is based on a fish fillet that's 1 to 1½ inches thick. If you have a much thinner piece of fish, decrease the cooking time to 20 minutes.

INGREDIENTS

FISH

4 (6- to 7-ounce/170- to 200-g) skinless cod fillets, 1 to 1½ inches thick

Salt and pepper

¼ cup/60 ml coconut milk

COCONUT BROTH

2 cups/475 ml fish or chicken stock

2 cups/475 ml coconut milk

2 stalks lemongrass, white part only, cut in half and bruised

4 kaffir lime leaves, torn

4 thick slices galangal (or ginger if you can't get galangal)

2 teaspoons/10 ml fish sauce

2 teaspoons/10 ml lime juice

2 teaspoons palm sugar/4 g or firmly packed light brown sugar

2 small fresh red chiles, bruised

GARNISH

¼ cup/13 g cilantro leaves

4 small fresh red chiles, seeded and chopped

DIRECTIONS

Preheat a sous vide water bath to 131°F/55°C.

To make the fish, season the cod fillets with salt and pepper, place each in its own vacuum-seal bag, and pour 1 tablespoon of coconut milk into each bag. Seal the bags. Cook in the preheated water bath for 30 minutes.

With about 20 minutes of cooking time left on the fish, make the broth. Combine the fish stock, coconut milk, lemongrass, kaffir lime leaves, and galangal in a pot over high heat. Bring to a boil, then decrease the heat to low and simmer the broth for 10 minutes.

When the fish has 3 to 5 minutes left of sous vide cooking, add the fish sauce, lime juice, sugar, and chile to the broth, simmer for a few more minutes, and then remove from the heat.

Carefully transfer the fish from the vacuum-seal bags to serving bowls (it will be quite delicate). Strain the broth and pour over the fish into the bowls. Garnish with the cilantro and chile.

Stuffing your own rice paper rolls gives you a certain sense of satisfaction, and it's a great family activity that the kids will love. The recipe below is delicious, but feel free to get creative with the fillings and add your favorite veggies as well. The best part is that they look far more difficult to make than they actually are!

SHRIMP SUMMER ROLLS

🌡 135°F/57°C | ⏱ 15 MINUTES | 🍴 SERVES 4 (3 ROLLS EACH)

INGREDIENTS

18 medium-size shrimp (about 1½ shrimp per roll), raw, peeled, and deveined

PEANUT DIPPING SAUCE

1 tablespoon/15 ml dark soy sauce

¼ cup/60 ml hoisin sauce

2 tablespoons/30 g chili garlic sauce

2 garlic cloves, minced

6 tablespoons/90 g peanut butter

10 tablespoons/150 ml warm water

RICE PAPER ROLLS

12 rice paper sheets

24 fresh mint leaves

24 (4-inch/10-cm) segments of spring onion

1½ ounces/43 g vermicelli noodles, cooked, drained, and rinsed in cold water

12 butter lettuce leaves

10 small red chiles, chopped (optional, to garnish)

1 lime, cut into wedges

DIRECTIONS

Preheat a sous vide water bath to 135°F/57°C.

Lay the shrimp flat in vacuum-seal bags and cook in the preheated water bath for 15 minutes. Meanwhile, to make the dipping sauce, combine all of the ingredients in a small bowl, cover, and refrigerate.

When the shrimp has finished cooking sous vide, plunge the bag into an ice water bath for 5 to 10 minutes. When cool, remove the shrimp from the vacuum-seal bag, discarding any liquid, and slice each shrimp in half lengthwise.

To make the rolls, dip one rice paper wrapper into warm water until softened (approximately 10 seconds). Remove the wrapper from the water and place on a clean surface. Place 3 shrimp halves, 2 mint leaves, and 2 spring onion segments on the wrapper. Tightly wrap about 1½ tablespoons of noodles in a leaf of lettuce to form a log shape, and place on top of the shrimp on the wrapper. Fold in the sides of the wrapper, followed by the bottom of the wrapper. Roll up tightly to form a spring roll shape. (See the folding guide on the oposite page.) Repeat the process with the remaining wrappers and filling.

To serve, arrange the rolls on a plate and scatter the chile over the top. Portion out the dipping sauce into individual sauce bowls. Serve with lime wedges.

This take on Vietnamese rolls (bánh mì) features tender sous vide chicken. To make it as close as possible to the sandwich you'd find at a Vietnamese restaurant, you'll need freshly baked crusty baguettes along with pickled carrot and daikon. We'll handle the chicken and pickles in this recipe, so you'll just need to find the best bread you can to go with them. You can also replace the chicken with roasted or sous vide pork belly slices, such as the Sticky Pork Belly on page 206.

SHREDDED CHICKEN BÁNH MÌ

🌡 140°F/60°C | ⏱ 1¼ HOURS | 🍴 SERVES 4

INGREDIENTS

4 skinless, boneless chicken breasts

PICKLED CARROT AND DAIKON

1 cup/240 ml water

½ cup/120 ml rice vinegar

½ cup/100 g sugar

1 teaspoon/6 g salt

1 medium carrot, peeled and julienned

8 ounces/230 g daikon (or young turnip or radish if you can't find daikon), peeled and julienned

BÁNH MÌ

1 to 2 tablespoons/15 to 30 ml Maggi seasoning or soy sauce, or to taste

1 to 2 tablespoons/15 to 30 ml chili sauce, such as Sriracha, or to taste

4 fresh individual baguettes or 1 long (26 inches) baguette

2-inch/5-cm piece of cucumber, thinly sliced

16 sprigs cilantro

2 tablespoons/28 g mayonnaise

1 to 2 tablespoons chopped jalapeño, or to taste

DIRECTIONS

Preheat a sous vide water bath to 140°F/60°C.

Seal the chicken breasts in vacuum-seal bags (1 or 2 per bag depending on the size of your bags) and cook in the preheated water bath for 1 hour 15 minutes.

To make the pickled carrot and daikon, combine the water, vinegar, sugar, and salt in a medium-size bowl and whisk until the sugar and salt are dissolved. Add the carrot and daikon to the pickling brine, then cover and refrigerate.

To make the bánh mì, when the chicken has finished cooking sous vide, remove it from the vacuum-seal bags and shred it with two forks. Place in a bowl, add the Maggi seasoning or soy and chili sauce to taste, and toss to combine. Drain the pickling brine from the veggies, and reserve the pickled vegetables.

Paint your baguettes with mayonnaise, and fill with the cucumber, dressed chicken, pickled veggies and finally cilantro. To spice it up, top with some chopped jalapeño.

Inspired by celebrity chef Nobu Matsuhisa's miso cod, this dish gives a simple cod fillet a bit of panache. The marinade works in two ways: to tenderize and to add flavor. The result is a seriously tasty fillet that's infused with the delicious Japanese flavors of sake and miso. I recommend letting the fish be the star when you serve this, so pair it with some simple steamed Asian greens, rice, and spring onions.

MISO-MARINATED BLACK COD

☼ 131°F/55°C | 🕐 30 MINUTES (SEE NOTE) | ✗ SERVES 4

Note: The timing in this recipe is based on a fish fillet that's 1 to 1½ inches thick. If you have a much thinner piece of fish, decrease the cooking time to 20 minutes.

INGREDIENTS

¼ cup/60 ml sake

¼ cup/60 ml mirin

2 tablespoons/35 g white miso paste

3 tablespoons/37 g sugar

4 (7-ounce/200-g) skinless black cod fillets, 1 to 1½ inches/2 to 4 cm thick

Vegetable oil (optional, if finishing on the stove)

DIRECTIONS

In a small pot over medium-high heat, bring the sake and mirin to a boil. Decrease the heat to medium and whisk in the miso paste and sugar until they're dissolved and the mixture has a uniform consistency, about 1 minute. Pour the sauce into a resealable plastic bag and plunge it into an ice bath to cool. Once the sauce is cool, add the cod fillets to the bag with the marinade and store it in the fridge overnight.

The next day, preheat a sous vide water bath to 131°F/55°C.

Drop the plastic bag into the preheated water bath, seal using the displacement method (see page 14), clip the bag to the side of the preheated water bath, and cook for 30 minutes.

When the cod fillets have finished cooking sous vide, carefully remove them from the vacuum-seal bags (they're very delicate), reserving the liquid. Tip the liquid into a pan to reduce for a few moments, then remove from the heat. Lightly wipe off the excess marinade with paper towels, but don't remove it all. Now you have two options: if you have a blowtorch, use that to blacken the outside of the fish; otherwise, heat a skillet over high heat until it's very hot, add some vegetable oil, and then char the outside of the cod for 1 to 1½ minutes on each side, or until you get some good color (do this extremely carefully so the fish doesn't break).

With one side fried and one side steamed, gyoza are an addictive appetizer bite after bite. This is not the easiest of recipes, but you really do get a great sense of satisfaction when you've made your very own little gyoza—including the dough for the wrappers. However, if you're not feeling up for making your own dumpling wrappers, don't feel bad about buying premade ones. Likewise, I included a dipping sauce below, but if you have another favorite Asian sauce that you prefer, by all means go for that. Hoisin, sweet chili, and XO sauce all go well with this recipe.

DUCK GYOZA

🌡 135°F/57°C | ⏲ 2 HOURS | 🍴 MAKES 24 GYOZA, SERVES 6

INGREDIENTS

SOUS VIDE DUCK

1 skinless duck breast

GYOZA WRAPPERS

2 cups/240 g all-purpose flour, plus more for dusting

¼ teaspoon/1.7 g salt

½ cup/120 ml just-boiled water

GYOZA FILLING

3 shiitake mushrooms, boiled until tender, about 3 to 4 minutes, diced

2 teaspoons/3 g minced ginger

2 garlic cloves, minced

1 tablespoon/9 g minced onion

2 teaspoons/10 ml rice vinegar

1 teaspoon/5 ml light soy sauce

2 teaspoons/6 ml sesame oil

Salt and black pepper

DIPPING SAUCE

¼ cup/60 ml light soy sauce

3 tablespoons/45 ml black vinegar

2 tablespoons/30 ml chile oil, or to taste

FOR FRYING

3 tablespoons/45 ml peanut oil or vegetable oil, divided

¼ cup/60 ml water, divided

Note: The black vinegar used here is a dark, complex vinegar available at Asian supermarkets.

DIRECTIONS

Preheat a sous vide water bath to 135°F/57°C.

To make the sous vide duck, seal the duck breast in a vacuum-seal bag and cook in the preheated water bath for 2 hours.

To make the gyoza wrappers, sift the flour and salt into a bowl. Slowly add the water just off the boil, stirring with chopsticks or a fork until you can form the mixture into a ball. Cover the ball with a damp cloth and let it sit at room temperature for 1 hour. Knead the dough until smooth, about 5 minutes, then form it into a log. Using a sharp knife, cut the log into approximately ½-inch/1-cm slices. Roll out each slice into a thin sheet with a rolling pin and dust with flour (otherwise they will stick together and all your hard work will go to waste!). Using a circular cookie cutter, burger ring, or a similar shaped tool of about 3½ inches/9 cm, cut out circles from the dough. Gather the scraps together and roll and cut more wrappers. You should get about 24 wrappers.

To make the filling, combine all of the ingredients in a nonstick skillet and fry for a 3 to 4 minutes, until fragrant. Transfer to a large bowl.

To make the dipping sauce, combine the ingredients in a small bowl.

Once the duck has finished cooking, remove it from the bag and finely dice. Add the diced duck to the gyoza filling mixture.

Begin folding a gyoza by following the folding guide (see opposite page), filling each wrapper with 1 heaping teaspoon of filling. Repeat until you have filled all the gyoza.

To fry the gyoza, heat 1½ tablespoons of the peanut oil in a wok over medium heat. Add half the folded gyoza to the pan, then add 2 tablespoons of the water and cover the wok. Allow the dumplings to steam for 3 minutes. Remove the cover and fry until the bottoms have browned, about 2 minutes. Serve the first batch of gyoza.

Repeat the steaming and frying process with the remaining 1½ tablespoons oil, remaining half of the gyoza, and remaining 2 tablespoons water. Serve with the dipping or an Asian dipping sauce of your choice.

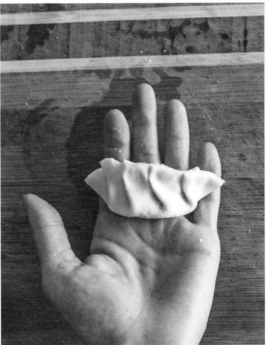

People often get put off making their own ramen because it seems too difficult and there are too many choices. So I've devised a three-step system for ramen making that allows you to easily personalize the ramen to your taste, preferred difficulty level, and amount of time you want to spend making it. Just choose your toppings, your broth, and your noodles, and then you're ready to get cooking! Sure, the pork belly takes 24 hours, but it's sous vide, so you'll hardly spend any active time. And if you're pressed for time you can sub in the Char Siu Chinese Barbecue Pork Loin on page 176. Okay, let's get cooking. Welcome to my ramen workshop!

RAMEN WITH STICKY PORK BELLY

✕ SERVES 4

This pork belly takes 24 hours, or 48 if you want to brine it, too (for brining instructions, see my recipe on page 86), so you'll want to get this started first. The reward for the investment of time is pork that's super juicy: the fat and tough fibers have softened with 24 hours of cooking in char siu marinade.

Step 1: The Sticky Pork Belly (and Other Toppings)

🌡 158°F/70°C | 🕐 24 HOURS

INGREDIENTS

2 pounds/900 g pork belly, excess fat from the top layer trimmed

1 cup/240 ml Char Siu Marinade (page 176)

DIRECTIONS

Preheat a sous vide water bath to 158°F/70°C.

Brush the pork belly with half the marinade, seal in a vacuum-seal bag, and cook in the preheated water bath for 24 hours.

When the pork has finished cooking sous vide, preheat a broiler to the highest setting. Paint a layer of the marinade over the pork and transfer it, skin-side up, to a foil-lined baking tray. Place it under the broiler for 5 minutes, or until the marinade begins to caramelize and bubble. At this point, remove the pork from the broiler and brush

it again with the marinade. Either torch the top with a blowtorch or broil for another 5 minutes, or long enough to get a nicely caramelized surface.

When you're done with the blowtorch or when you've removed the pork from the oven, slice and serve immediately.

There are so many additional toppings you can use for ramen, and they're largely up to your personal taste. To keep things simple, I've listed just a few of the most popular toppings below. I recommend between 3 and 8 toppings total.

SECONDARY TOPPING IDEAS

INGREDIENTS

Scallion (a must for all ramen, in my opinion!)

Menma (fermented bamboo shoots)

Nori sheets (seaweed sheets)

Pickled vegetables

Sous vide eggs (see pages 19 to 20)

Narutomaki slices (those white slices of Japanese fish cake with a pink swirl)

Cooked shiitake or beech mushrooms

Fried bacon, chopped into small strips

Cooked sweet corn

Burnt garlic oil

Chile oil

Red pepper flakes

Step 2: The Broth

- Tonkotsu Pork Broth (12 hours)
- Chicken Miso Broth (10 minutes)
- Dashi "From the Sea" Broth (25 minutes)

For many, tonkotsu pork broth is the king (or queen) of the ramen broths. Pork bones are cooked for so long that the collagen melts and the broth becomes almost thick. For a soup base that isn't so involved, you can opt for the chicken miso broth. It takes just 10 minutes, and is lighter in both color and flavor than the pork broth. For seafood lovers, there's a third option as well. The dashi "from the sea" broth is made by boiling kelp, and it comes together in just under a half hour. All three of these broth recipes make 4 servings but can be doubled or tripled if you want to make extra and freeze it for future ramen.

TONKOTSU PORK BROTH (12 HOURS)

INGREDIENTS

4½ pounds/2 kg pork bones, such as pig's trotters, smoked hock, and thigh bones (a mix of cuts is good)

2 pounds/900 g chicken bones

1 gallon (4 L) plus 2 cups (475 ml) water

4 slices bacon

2 cups/480 ml chicken stock

6-inch/15-cm piece of ginger, thinly sliced

2 onions, halved, charred for a couple of minutes in a hot dry skillet

2 whole bulbs garlic, cloves separated, peeled, and roughly chopped

2 carrots, roughly chopped

3 leeks, roughly chopped

15 scallions, ends removed, halved

2 green apples, quartered

ADDITIONAL FLAVORINGS

1 tablespoon/15 ml soy sauce

2 teaspoons/10 ml sesame oil

2 teaspoons/10 ml rice vinegar

1 tablespoon/15 ml sake

Salt and pepper to taste

1 teaspoon to 1 tablespoon/1 to 2 g red pepper flakes, to taste (optional)

DIRECTIONS

To make the broth, place all the bones in a large pot, cover with water, and let rest for 1 hour (note that this water will not be the water you use for the broth; it will only be used to rinse the bones and then it will be discarded). After 1 hour, place the pot over high heat. Just before the water boils, take the pot off the heat, strain the bones into a large colander, and discard the water. Wash the bones under the cold running water to remove any blood or meat pieces. Add the water to the pot, put the clean bones back in, and bring the water to a boil. Cover the pot, decrease the heat to maintain a strong simmer, and simmer for 6 hours, skimming any scum off the top every now and again. After 6 hours, add the bacon, chicken stock, ginger, onions, garlic, carrots, leeks, scallions, and green apples and simmer for 5 hours longer.

Strain the broth so that there are no solid pieces in it, then return the liquid to the pot, checking to see that you have 8 cups of stock. If not, add more water. Then add the flavorings: soy sauce, sesame oil, rice vinegar, sake, salt and pepper, and red pepper flakes. Simmer for 5 to 10 more minutes and then your broth is ready. Set it aside as you prepare the rest of the ramen recipe.

CHICKEN MISO BROTH (10 MINUTES)

INGREDIENTS

8 cups/2 L chicken stock

¾ tablespoon/13 g white miso paste

1 tablespoon/15 ml white soy sauce or light soy sauce

1 teaspoon/5 ml sake

4 teaspoons/20 ml sesame oil

½ teaspoon/2 g sugar

¼ cup/60 ml unsweetened soy milk

DIRECTIONS

Bring the chicken stock to a boil in a pot over high heat. Add the miso, soy sauce, sake, sesame oil, and sugar and boil for 5 to 10 minutes, or until the concentration of flavor is to your liking.

Remove from the heat and stir in the soy milk. The broth is ready. Set it aside as you prepare the rest of the ramen recipe.

DASHI "FROM THE SEA" BROTH (25 MINUTES)

INGREDIENTS

8 sheets kombu (dried kelp)

8 cups/2 L pork stock (or fish stock to keep it pescatarian)

2 teaspoons/10 ml rice wine vinegar

½ teaspoon/2 g sugar

3 tablespoons/45 ml soy sauce

1 teaspoon/5 ml sake

DIRECTIONS

In a large pot, combine the kombu and pork stock and bring to a boil over high heat. Boil for 15 to 20 minutes, or until you can taste a good amount of the kelp flavor in the soup, then remove the kombu sheets. Add the rice wine vinegar, sugar, sauce, and sake, stir well, and simmer for 5 to 10 minutes, or until the concentration of flavor is to your liking. The broth is ready. Set it aside as you prepare the rest of the ramen recipe.

Step 3: The Noodles

For four people, you'll need four servings of ramen noodles. I recommend using a Japanese brand of either long, straight-style ramen noodles (dried or fresh) or wavy-style ramen noodles (dried or fresh). Straight-style ramen noodles usually come in bundles separated into serving sizes, and there are often two servings per packet. They have a cleaner, smoother mouthfeel. Wavy-style noodles, on the other hand, have a chewier texture. Most of the run-of-the-mill dried noodles that you see on the supermarket shelves are of the wavy variety. I use both kinds of noodles depending on what mood I'm in, but the long, straight-style noodles are my favorite for a good, classic ramen.

Assembling each bowl is up to you depending on the ingredients, but the base for each bowl will be one nest of noodles with about 2 cups/475 ml of broth.

Sous vide scrambled eggs have a silky, just-cooked texture. Unlike cooking scrambled eggs in a pan or pot—where there are usually certain parts that are cooked perfectly, while some areas are undercooked or overcooked—these eggs are wonderfully uniform. With the addition of both cream and butter, these eggs are rich and creamy as well. If you wanted to make them a bit healthier, you can substitute whole or skim milk for the cream and reduce the amount of butter. Check the eggs after 30 minutes, if they need longer or you'd prefer them to be cooked more, leave them in for another 10 minutes or so.

INDULGENT SCRAMBLED EGGS

🌡 167°F/75°C | ⏲ 30 MINUTES | 🍴 SERVES 4

INGREDIENTS

12 eggs, at room temperature

¼ cup/60 ml cream

4 tablespoons/56 g unsalted butter, melted

Salt and black pepper

Very small handful of fresh chives or parsley, to serve

4 to 8 slices of toasted rye bread, to serve

DIRECTIONS

Preheat a sous vide water bath to 167°F/75°C.

Whisk the eggs, cream, and butter together in a bowl along with a generous pinch of salt. Seal using the displacement method (see page 14), clip the bag to the edge of your preheated water bath, and cook for 15 minutes. Unclip the bag and give the eggs a gentle stir with a spoon to ensure even cooking (be careful not to overstir, though, or the eggs can become mushy). Return to the bath as before, displacing the air from the bag, and cook for an additional 15 minutes.

When the eggs are done cooking, open the bag and give them another gentle stir to loosen them from the bag. Pour them gently onto serving plates. Scatter over some chives, add salt and pepper to taste, and serve with rye bread or the bread of your choice.

This recipe uses the same technique as the Indulgent Scrambled Eggs (page 215), but it adds smoked salmon to the mix. I think you'll find the saltiness and smokiness of the salmon makes it a perfect match for creamy sous vide eggs. Because the salmon is kept in the fridge until cooking, it will bring the temperature down—so I recommend cooking the eggs a bit longer in this recipe.

SALMON AND EGGS ON A BAGEL

🌡 167°F/75°C | ⏱ 35 MINUTES | 🍴 SERVES 4

INGREDIENTS

12 eggs, at room temperature

¼ cup/56 g sour cream

¼ cup/60 ml heavy cream

4 tablespoons/56 g unsalted butter, melted

½ cup/70 g smoked salmon, sliced into slivers

2 bagels, halved

2 tablespoons/10 g chopped fresh chives

Sea salt and freshly cracked pepper

DIRECTIONS

Preheat a sous vide water bath to 167°F/75°C.

Whisk together the eggs, sour cream, heavy cream, and butter in a large bowl, then mix in the salmon. Pour the mixture into a resealable bag, seal using the displacement method (see page 14), clip the bag to the edge of the preheated water bath, and cook for 17 minutes.

Unclip the bag and give the eggs a gentle stir with a spoon to ensure even cooking (be careful not to overstir, though, or the eggs can become mushy). Return to the bath as before, displacing the air from the bag, and cook for an additional 18 minutes.

When the eggs are almost done, toast your bagel halves and place them on plates. You may want to put a napkin under the bagel halves as you plate to absorb any moisture that drips through from the eggs.

When the eggs are done cooking, open the bag and give them another gentle stir to loosen them from the bag. Pour them gently over the top of the bagel halves, scatter chives over the top, and season with sea salt and freshly cracked pepper. Remove the napkin before serving.

This sous vide preparation is inspired by the texture of a frittata: you'll make perfectly delicate and light eggs inside these pots, but you won't have the burnt or crispy edge of a traditional frittata. However, browned chorizo will give you some of the same flavor notes, and the robust flavors of the Cheddar, onion, tomato, and chives are sure to wow your brunch crowd.

CHEESY CHORIZO "FRITTATA"

🌡 176°F/80°C | ⏱ 1 HOUR | 🍴 SERVES 4

INGREDIENTS

1 tablespoon/15 ml vegetable oil

¾ cup/60 g sliced chorizo

¼ cup/36 g finely diced white onion

6 eggs

⅓ cup/80 ml milk

1 cup/113 g grated Cheddar cheese

6 cherry tomatoes, cut into quarters

Salt and black pepper to taste

3 tablespoons/45 g cream cheese

Chopped fresh chives, to garnish

Note: For this recipe you'll need 4 4-ounce/120 ml canning jars.

DIRECTIONS

Preheat a sous vide water bath to 176°F/80°C.

Heat a medium skillet over medium heat and add the oil. Fry the chorizo and onion until the onion is soft and the chorizo has browned, about 5 minutes, then remove from the heat. Crack the eggs into a large bowl and whisk well. Add the milk, grated cheese, cherry tomatoes, and salt and pepper to taste and whisk to combine. Fold in the chorizo and onion and whisk lightly.

Divide the mixture among the 4 glass pots or jars, spoon 3 small dollops of cream cheese on top of each, and put the lid on. Using tongs to hold the sides, and a spatula to support the weight, carefully place the pots or jars upright in the preheated water bath and cook for 1 hour.

After 1 hour, take the pots out of the water bath and remove the lids. Sprinkle some chopped chives over the top and serve immediately.

An omelet can be ruined just as easily as a steak when you're cooking with a frying pan. There may be no gray band of meat, but the texture of overcooked eggs is not any more pleasant. With sous vide, you get uniform cooking and avoid any rubbery eggs. The trick is to get the outside texture of a traditional omelet. We'll do that here in a similar way to the steak: searing the eggs quickly in a hot pan after sous vide.

BACON AND CHEESE OMELET

♨ 167°F/75°C | 🕐 25 MINUTES | ✗ SERVES 4

INGREDIENTS

¼ cup roughly chopped bacon plus 2 tablespoons finely chopped bacon, divided

12 large eggs, at room temperature

½ cup/56 g grated aged Cheddar cheese

2 tablespoons/30 ml whole milk

2 tablespoons/30 ml cream

Unsalted butter, for the pan

¼ cup/10 g chopped fresh chives

Black pepper

DIRECTIONS

Preheat a sous vide water bath to 167°F/75°C.

In a large frying pan over medium heat, fry the 2 tablespoons of roughly chopped bacon, stirring occasionally, until the bacon is browned and crisp, 5 to 10 minutes.

Crack the eggs into a bowl, add the cheese, milk, cream, and cooked bacon, and whisk until just combined, then transfer to 2 resealable plastic bags. Seal using the displacement method (see page 14), clip the bags to the side of the preheated water bath, and cook for 25 minutes. Halfway through cooking, unclip the bags and give the eggs a stir, then return the bags to the water bath.

Place the remaining 2 tablespoons finely chopped bacon in the frying pan and fry over medium heat until browned and crisp, 5 to 10 minutes. Spread on a paper towel to drain.

When the eggs are finished cooking sous vide, make sure the frying pan is preheated over medium heat. Butter the pan, then remove one bag of eggs, give the eggs a gentle stir to loosen them from the bag, then tip them out of the bag into the skillet for a quick sear. Push the omelet into the corner of the skillet with a spatula, and shape with a spoon as needed. Because it's already cooked, you only need to brown the surface, then flip and brown the other side if you'd like (you can leave one side as is for a moister omelet).

Transfer the omelet to two plates and top with the chives, bacon bits, and black pepper. Repeat this process for the second omelet for two.

While some swear you can cook hollandaise sous vide, I've found the texture is never quite right. It's a sauce that simply has to be whisked. However, sous vide can keep the eggs hands-free, which lets you focus on whisking the perfect sauce! For the eggs in this recipe, I recommend cooking at 147°F/64°C for 45 minutes. The yolks will set a bit, yet they're still loose enough to mop up with English muffins.

EGGS BENEDICT

🌡 147°F/64°C | 🕐 45 MINUTES | 🍴 SERVES 4

INGREDIENTS

8 eggs, at room temperature

4 English muffins, halved

1 tablespoon chopped fresh chives

HOLLANDAISE

4 egg yolks

3 tablespoons/45 ml white vinegar

8 tablespoons/113 g unsalted butter, melted

Sea salt and white pepper

DIRECTIONS

Preheat a sous vide water bath to 147°F/64°C.

Using a ladle, carefully lower the 8 eggs (still in their shell) into the water bath and cook for 45 minutes. When they're finished cooking, put the eggs into a bowl of warm water and carefully remove the shells (see page 20 for more on this technique).

About 20 minutes before the eggs finish cooking, bring a small pot of water to a simmer. You'll want a pot size that works with a small metal mixing bowl, as you'll place the bowl on top of the simmering pot to apply the right amount of heat while you make the hollandaise.

To make the hollandaise, 5 to 10 minutes before the eggs are finished, your water should be at a simmer. Place a heatproof bowl on top of the simmering pot, then add 4 raw egg yolks and 3 tablespoons of white vinegar. Whisk continuously for a couple of minutes. Then, while continuing to whisk with one hand, slowly pour in the melted butter with the other hand, continually whisking this whole time. Add salt and white pepper and whisk just a bit more until the mixture reaches the desired consistency. Turn off the heat and set aside. If it gets too thick, you can whisk in a small amount of water.

Right before the eggs have finished cooking sous vide, toast your muffins. Plate the muffins, remove the eggs from the sous vide container, and peel. Place the eggs on top of the muffins—depress the muffins if you want to make sure the eggs sit on them nicely. Then spoon hollandaise over the top, and scatter the chives.

It's not always feasible to have a tasty and nutritious breakfast when you're pressed for time in the morning. That's one reason why this overnight oatmeal is a winner. Enjoy one of these recipes as is or make it your own. Top with apple slices, blueberries, granola, nuts, seeds, or coconut chips . . . the combinations are endless!

OVERNIGHT OATMEAL

❄ 180°F/82°C | ⏱ 6 TO 10 HOURS | ✖ SERVES 4

INGREDIENTS

SIMPLE OATMEAL

2 cups/200 g rolled oats

6 cups (1,425 ml) water or milk

Sugar

Pinch of ground cinnamon

COCONUT AND BANANA OATMEAL

2 cups/200 g rolled oats

3 cups (700 ml) coconut milk

3 cups (700 ml) skimmed milk or water

3 bananas, mashed

1 teaspoon/5 ml vanilla extract

BLUEBERRY AND HONEY OATMEAL

1 cup/100 g rolled oats

⅔ cup/113 g blueberries

4 teaspoons/24 ml honey

Pinch of ground cinnamon

3 cups (700 ml) skim milk or water

3 bananas, mashed

1 teaspoon/5 ml vanilla extract

DIRECTIONS

Preheat a sous vide water bath to 180°F/82°C.

Combine all of the ingredients for the recipe of your choice in a resealable plastic bag. Seal using the displacement method (see page 14), clip the bag to the side of the preheated water bath, and cook overnight, or for 6 to 10 hours.

When the oatmeal is done, pour it out of the bag into serving bowls and add your toppings. You can refrigerate it to serve later; simply heat it up again in a pot over medium heat and add more milk as required.

Any day that starts with pancakes is a good day in my book! The only thing better is a plate of pancakes served with a delicious fresh compote. In fact, these compotes are so good they shouldn't be limited to pancakes. They're fantastic on waffles or a bowl of oatmeal as well as in smoothies and as a topping for desserts (like the cheesecake on page 245).

PANCAKES WITH FRUIT COMPOTES

♨ 185°F/85°C | ⏱ 1 HOUR | 🍴 SERVES 4

Blueberry Compote

INGREDIENTS

1 cup/170 g fresh blueberries, divided

2 tablespoons/30 ml honey

1 tablespoon/15 ml lemon juice

½ teaspoon/2½ ml vanilla extract

2 tablespoons/30 ml water mixed with ½ tablespoon/3¾ g cornstarch

DIRECTIONS

Preheat a sous vide water bath to 185°F/85°C.

Combine ½ cup/85 g of the blueberries with the honey, lemon juice, and vanilla in a resealable plastic bag. Slowly stir in the water and cornstarch mixture until combined. Seal using the displacement method (see page 14), clip the bag to the side of the preheated water bath, and cook for 30 minutes.

Open the bag, add the remaining ½ cup/85 g blueberries, reseal the bag as before, and cook for another 30 minutes. When the second 30 minutes is up, remove the bag but don't open it yet. Use a spatula to squash the blueberries through the bag until they reach a consistency you're happy with. Open the bag and serve immediately, or transfer to a small bowl and microwave if you want an even hotter compote.

Strawberry Compote

INGREDIENTS

1 cup/167 g fresh strawberries, divided

1 tablespoon/15 ml lemon juice

2 tablespoons/25 g sugar

2 tablespoons/30 ml water mixed with ½ tablespoon/ 3¾ g cornstarch

DIRECTIONS

Preheat a sous vide water bath to 185°F/85°C.

Combine ½ cup of the strawberries with the lemon juice and sugar in a resealable plastic bag. Slowly stir in the water and cornstarch mixture until combined. Seal using the displacement method (see page 14), clip the bag to the side of the preheated water bath, and cook for 30 minutes.

Open the bag, add the remaining ½ cup strawberries, reseal the bag as before, and cook for another 30 minutes. When the second 30 minutes is up, remove the bag but don't open it yet. Use a spatula to squash the strawberries through the bag until they reach a consistency you're happy with. Open the bag and serve immediately, or transfer to a small bowl and microwave if you want an even hotter compote.

Lemon Compote

INGREDIENTS

3 lemons

¼ cup/50 g sugar

½ teaspoon/2½ ml vanilla extract

DIRECTIONS

Preheat a sous vide water bath to 185°F/85°C.

Zest the 3 lemons into a bowl, taking care not to remove any white pith. Juice the lemons into the same bowl, then stir in the sugar to combine. Transfer the mixture to a resealable plastic bag. Seal using the displacement method (see page 14), clip the bag to the side of the preheated water bath, and cook for 1 hour. When the time is up, transfer the mixture to a blender and pulse a few times until you have a uniform but chunky mixture. Serve immediately, or transfer to a small bowl and microwave if you want a hotter compote.

Pancakes

INGREDIENTS

1 cup/120 g all-purpose flour

2 tablespoons/25 g sugar

1 teaspoon/5 g baking powder

½ teaspoon/2½ g baking soda

½/3 g teaspoon salt

¾ to 1 cup/180 to 240 ml milk (more for thinner pancakes, less for extra fluffy)

2 tablespoons/28 g unsalted butter, melted, plus extra solid butter for cooking

1 egg

1 teaspoon/5 ml vanilla extract

Confectioners' sugar, for dusting (optional)

DIRECTIONS

Sift together the flour, sugar, baking powder, baking soda, and salt into a medium-size mixing bowl. In a large bowl, whisk together ¾ cup (180 ml) of the milk and the melted butter, egg, and vanilla extract. Whisk in the flour mixture bit by bit until well combined and free of any lumps. If the batter is too thick, add some extra milk.

Heat a wide, heavy-bottomed frying pan over medium heat. Coat the pan well with butter and cook the pancakes one at a time, wiping the frying pan with paper towels after every couple of pancakes to remove the burnt butter.

Top with the compote of your choice and dust with confectioners' sugar.

Just like Overnight Oatmeal (page 224), this is a dish to start just before you go to bed. Then it will be perfectly cooked and waiting for you in the morning. No more rushed breakfasts thrown together while you run out the door! If you want to make this dish a bit healthier, you can toast the pecans in a dry pan instead of making candied pecans.

BREAKFAST QUINOA WITH CANDIED PECANS AND BERRIES

🌡* 180°F/82°C | 🕐 6 TO 10 HOURS OR OVERNIGHT | 🍴 SERVES 4

INGREDIENTS

QUINOA

2 cups (475 ml) almond milk

1 cup/177 g quinoa, rinsed and drained

¼ teaspoon ground cinnamon

1 teaspoon/5 ml vanilla extract

3 tablespoons/45 ml honey

2 cups/220 g blackberries, divided

CANDIED PECANS

1 tablespoon/14 g unsalted butter

½ cup/57 g pecans, halved

1 tablespoon/11½ g firmly packed brown sugar

DIRECTIONS

Preheat a sous vide water bath to 180°F/82°C.

To make the quinoa, combine the almond milk, quinoa, cinnamon, vanilla, honey, and ½ cup/55 g of the blackberries in a resealable plastic bag. Seal using the displacement method (see page 14), clip the bag to the side of the preheated water bath, and cook for 6 to 10 hours (or overnight).

Meanwhile, before you go to bed, make the candied pecans. Melt the butter in a saucepan over medium-high heat. Add the pecans and stir to coat in the butter. Add the sugar and stir until caramelized, about 5 minutes. Transfer to parchment paper to cool.

When the quinoa has finished cooking sous vide, empty the contents of the bag into a large bowl and add half of the pecans. Fluff the quinoa with two forks, then divide among individual serving bowls. Top with the remaining blackberries and candied pecans.

Note: Because steam cannot circulate through the bag like it can the way you may usually cook quinoa, the quinoa will not be as light and uniformly cooked as you may be used to. Think of it as more like an interesting alternative to porridge, with a slightly different texture and loads of protein and essential amino acids. When it's finished, tip out the loose contents into a bowl and fluff up to mix, leaving any hard, uncooked quinoa in the bag (it will naturally stick in there anyway).

If you've never tried rice for breakfast, keep an open mind. When you combine it with familiar breakfast flavors like banana, cinnamon, and honey, it won't seem strange at all. This is another recipe built to cook while you sleep, so it's very convenient. The only thing you'll have to do in the morning is make the caramelized bananas, which is super easy (especially if you've already had your coffee!).

CARAMELIZED BANANA AND BROWN RICE BOOSTER BOWL

♨ 180°F/82°C | ⏲ 6 TO 10 HOURS OR OVERNIGHT | ✗ SERVES 4 TO 6

INGREDIENTS

1 cup/200 g brown rice, rinsed and drained

3½ cups (820 ml) almond milk

¼ teaspoon/1 g ground cinnamon

3 tablespoons/45 ml honey

½ teaspoon/2½ ml vanilla extract

Pinch of salt

4 medium-size bananas, peeled and sliced ⅛ to ¼ inch/3 to 6 mm thick, divided, plus extra to serve

2 tablespoons/28 g unsalted butter

2 tablespoons/23 g firmly packed brown sugar

DIRECTIONS

Preheat a sous vide water bath to 180°F/82°C.

Combine the brown rice, almond milk, cinnamon, honey, vanilla, salt, and 2 of the sliced bananas in a resealable plastic bag. Seal using the displacement method (see page 14), clip the bag to the side of the preheated water bath, and cook for 6 to 10 hours or overnight.

Five to 10 minutes before serving, melt the butter and brown sugar in a pot over medium-high heat until bubbling. Place the remaining 2 sliced bananas flat and cook in the mixture for 2 minutes on each side, or until you get some good caramelization on the outside. When the bananas are done, transfer to parchment paper and let cool slightly.

When the brown rice has finished cooking sous vide, tip the contents of the bag into a large bowl. Mix the brown rice mixture with two forks, adding extra almond milk if required, then divide among individual serving bowls. Stir in some extra sliced fresh banana and top with the caramelized banana slices.

Note: Because steam cannot circulate through the bag like it can in a rice steamer, the rice will not be cooked in a totally uniform fashion. When it's finished, tip out the loose contents into a bowl and fluff with a fork to mix. Leave any hard, uncooked rice in the bag (it will naturally stick in there anyway).

This simple dessert makes pear the star of the dish. Over the hour cooking time, the pears become soft and infused with the delicious flavors of vanilla, star anise, and saffron. And because fruit is the key ingredient, you might be able to almost fool yourself into thinking it's healthy—almost.

SAFFRON, VANILLA, AND WHITE WINE PEARS

✶ 181°F/83°C　|　⏱ 1 HOUR　|　✗ SERVES 4

INGREDIENTS

⅓ cup (80 ml) white wine

1 tablespoon/15 ml freshly squeezed lemon juice

½ cup/100 g sugar (superfine is ideal)

½ teaspoon/2 ½ g saffron

1 star anise

1 vanilla bean, split lengthwise

4 pears, peeled, cored, and halved through the stem end

Mascarpone cheese, to serve

DIRECTIONS

Preheat a sous vide water bath to 181°F/83°C.

Whisk together the white wine, lemon juice, and sugar in a medium-size bowl until the sugar has mostly dissolved. Transfer the mixture to a large resealable plastic bag along with saffron, star anise, vanilla bean, and pears. Seal using the displacement method (see page 14), clip the bag to the side of the preheated water bath, and cook in for 1 hour.

Open the bag and tip the contents into a large bowl. Serve 2 pear halves in each of 4 serving bowls, along with a few spoonfuls of the liquid, and top with a dollop of mascarpone.

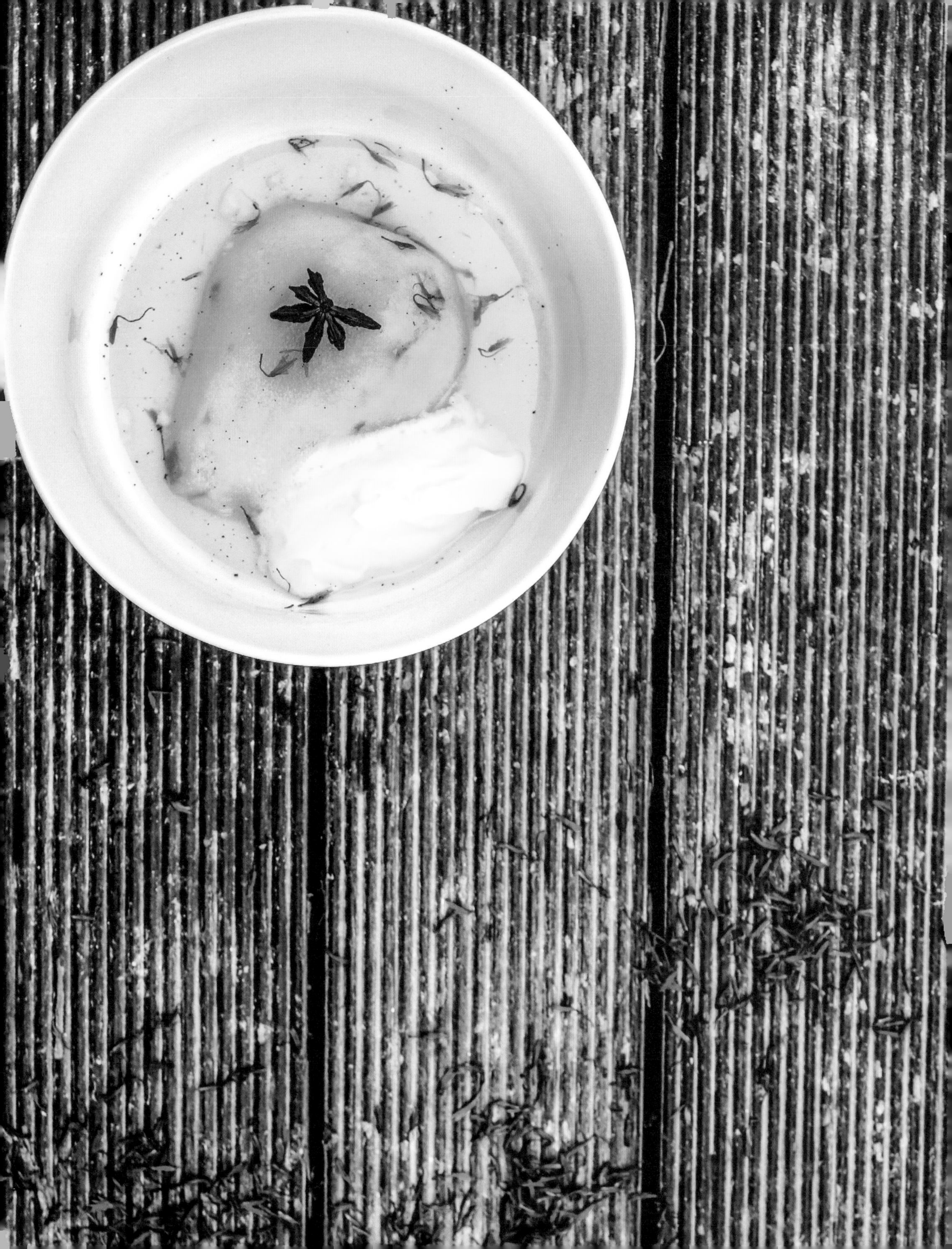

While the flavors here are inspired by the classic "American" apple pie, this pie filling is made with the magic of sous vide, which infuses flavors wonderfully fast and makes the whole process just a bit less messy. You'll also find this recipe includes a little cider, which adds a lovely depth of flavor. This filling is sweet, sticky, gooey, and delicious. As for the pie crust, I have included my recipe here, but you can certainly take a shortcut and use store-bought crust instead.

ALL-AMERICAN APPLE PIE

🌡 183°F/84°C | ⏱ 1 HOUR | ✗ MAKES 1 PIE, ABOUT 8 SERVINGS

INGREDIENTS

PIE CRUST

2½ cups/300 g all-purpose flour, plus more for dusting

½ teaspoon/3½ g salt

1 cup/226 g very cold unsalted butter, cubed

½ cup (120 ml) ice water

1 egg white, beaten

1 egg beaten with 2 tablespoons/30 ml milk

1 tablespoon/12½ g granulated sugar, for sprinkling

FILLING

8 tablespoons/113 g unsalted butter

3 tablespoons/22½ g all-purpose flour

½ cup/100 g granulated sugar

½ cup/100 g firmly packed brown sugar

¼ teaspoon/1 ¾ g ground cinnamon

¼ teaspoon/1¾ g salt

1 cup (240 ml) hard cider

2 tablespoons/30 ml freshly squeezed lemon juice

5½ cups/620 g peeled, cored, quartered and thinly sliced baking apples (I recommend using a mix of different types, such as Granny Smith, Honeycrisp, Mutsu, Crispin, Pink Lady, Golden Delicious, and Gala)

DIRECTIONS

If you choose to make the pie crust, start the recipe for the crust at least 2½ hours before the pie filling, or the day before. If using a store-bought crust, see the Note at the end of the recipe.

To make the crust, combine the flour and salt in a large bowl. Add the butter cubes and combine with a fork until you have coarse crumbs. Add the water 1 tablespoon at a time, stirring with a wooden spoon, until the dough forms a ball. Wrap the ball in plastic wrap and chill in the fridge for at least 4 hours or up to overnight.

If you're making the pie straight away, you can begin making the filling after 2½ hours (the filling takes about 1½ hours to prepare and cook, meaning that when it's finished, the pastry will have been in the fridge for 4 hours).

Preheat a sous vide water bath to 183°F/84°C.

Meanwhile, to make the filling, heat a large saucepan over medium heat and melt the butter. Stir in the flour until well combined, then add the sugars, cinnamon, salt, cider, and lemon juice and simmer until the mixture has reduced by half and becomes thick and syrupy, about 10 minutes. Pour the contents into a large resealable bag and add the sliced apples. Seal using the displacement method (see page 14), clip the bag to the edge of the preheated water bath, and cook for 1 hour.

Toward the end of the sous vide cooking, preheat the oven to 375°F/190°C. Divide the pie crust in half and roll out on a lightly floured surface (about ⅛ inch/3 mm thick, 13 inches/33 cm in diameter). Transfer it to a 9-inch/23-cm pie tin or dish and fit it inside. Roll out the second half in the same way. Slice into ¾-inch/2-cm–thick strips to form a lattice over the filling. Brush the bottom pie crust with the egg white and pour in your apple filling. Form the lattice over the top with the strips. Paint the top crust with the egg wash and sprinkle with the granulated sugar. Place the pie on a foil-lined baking sheet to catch any drips, transfer to the oven, and bake for 35 to 40 minutes, or until the crust is golden.

Note: If using store-bought crust, pour the apple filling into the pie crust and bake in the oven at 375°F/190°C for 35 to 40 minutes, or until the crust is golden.

Packed full of real pumpkin, this pie isn't just for Thanksgiving. Your whole family will start looking forward to this one as soon as the temperature cools. By using real pumpkin instead of the canned stuff, you'll know your pie is free of preservatives. And since you're cooking it sous vide, you'll also get all of the nutrition from the pumpkin (because you're not cooking it away at a high temperature).

SPICED PUMPKIN PIE

🌡 185°F/85°C | 🕐 1½ HOURS | 🍴 MAKES 1 PIE, ABOUT 8 SERVINGS

INGREDIENTS

PIE CRUST

1¼ cups/150 g all-purpose flour, plus more for dusting

¼ teaspoon salt

8 tablespoons/113 g very cold unsalted butter, cubed

¼ cup/60 ml very cold water

FILLING

5 cups/900 g peeled, diced pumpkin (roughly 1-inch/2.5-cm cubes)

¾ cup/180 ml evaporated milk

¾ cup/180 ml heavy cream

½ cup/107 g firmly packed brown sugar

¼ cup/50 g granulated sugar

¾ teaspoon ground cinnamon

1 teaspoon grated fresh ginger

¼ teaspoon freshly grated nutmeg

½ teaspoon salt

2 eggs

DIRECTIONS

To make the crust, combine the flour and salt in a large bowl. Add the butter cubes and combine with a fork until the mixture forms coarse crumbs. Add the water 1 tablespoon at a time, stirring with a wooden spoon, until the dough forms a ball. Wrap the ball in plastic wrap and chill in the fridge for at least 4 hours or up to overnight.

When you're ready to make the filling, preheat a sous vide water bath to 185°F/85°C.

To make the filling, place the pumpkin cubes flat in 1 or 2 vacuum-seal bags (depending on the size of your bags), seal, and cook in the preheated water bath for 1 hour 30 minutes.

When the pumpkin has finished cooking sous vide, remove from the water bath and preheat the oven to 375°F/191°C. In a large bowl, whisk together the evaporated milk, cream, both sugars, cinnamon, ginger, nutmeg, salt, and eggs until well combined. Push the pumpkin through a food mill or sieve until you have 2 cups (475 ml) of smooth purée and add it to the bowl. Use a handheld immersion blender or transfer the mixture to a food processor and blend until very smooth.

Remove your pie crust from the fridge and roll it out on a lightly floured surface about ¼ inch/5 mm thick and large enough to fit a 9-inch/23-cm pie dish. Transfer it to the pie dish and fit it inside. Pour in the pie filling and smooth the top with a rubber spatula. Place the pie on a foil-lined baking sheet to catch any drips, transfer to the oven, and bake until the center is almost set. The filling should still have some jiggle when you shake it, but a toothpick inserted 1 inch from the crust comes out clean, 55 to 60 minutes.

When it comes to cheesecake, the simplest recipes are often the best. This cheesecake uses just the classic ingredients, but cooks them in a novel way. The result is individual pots of cheesecake with that to-die-for creamy texture. Eat them as is, or top with a fruit topping like the Blueberry Compote (page 227).

NEW YORK CHEESECAKE POTS

🌡 176°F/80°C | ⏲ 1½ HOURS | 🍴 SERVES 4

INGREDIENTS

CHEESECAKE FILLING

10.6 ounces/300 g cream cheese

3 ounces/83 g sugar

½ teaspoon/2½ ml vanilla extract

1 egg, beaten

¾ cup/170 g sour cream

CHEESECAKE CRUST

4 tablespoons/56 g unsalted butter, melted

3½ ounces/100 g graham crackers

2 teaspoons/25 g white sugar

Butter, for greasing

Note: For this recipe you'll need 4 8-ounce/240 ml glass pots or canning jars

DIRECTIONS

Preheat a sous vide water bath to 176°F/80°C.

To make the filling, in a large bowl, mix together the cream cheese, sugar, and vanilla, then beat in the beaten egg, about half the egg at a time. Finally, mix in the sour cream and beat until smooth.

To make the crust, place all of the crust ingredients in a food processor and pulse a few times to combine. Grease four glass pots or canning jars with butter and then divide the crust mixture among the jars, packing it loosely at the bottom of each. Spoon the cheesecake filling evenly among the jars, layering it over the top of the crust. Seal the jars. Using tongs to hold the sides, and a spatula to support the weight, carefully place the pots or jars upright in the preheated water bath and cook for 1 hour 30 minutes.

Remove the pots from the water bath and set aside on the counter for 5 minutes (if you put the hot glass straight into an ice bath, the glass may break). After 5 minutes, plunge them into an ice bath for 5 to 10 minutes, then chill them in the fridge for a minimum of 4 hours, or ideally overnight, before serving.

I got the idea to try a sous vide lemon curd from a Melbourne chef friend of mine, and I'm so glad I did! You'll find this recipe has just the right amount of sourness from the lemons to balance the sweetness from the sugar. You can eat it on its own, use it in lemon tarts, dollop it on pancakes or muffins, and use it in so many other ways.

Before you make the recipe, I recommend rolling the lemons with your palm against the countertop to loosen the juices. Press down quite firmly as you roll them. You can feel when they are loosened enough because they will become noticeably softer. Also, if you're using a hand juicer, first put a kitchen cloth on the countertop, then a chopping board on top of that, and then place the juicer on top of the chopping board. This will do wonders for keeping the juicer in place as you twist the lemons.

LEMON CURD

🌡 167°F/75°C | ⏱ 1 HOUR | 🍴 MAKES 2 CUPS

INGREDIENTS

6 egg yolks

6 ounces/175 g sugar

⅓ teaspoon/.06 g gelatin powder

Small pinch of salt

7 ounces/200 g unsalted butter, melted

7 ounces/210 ml lemon juice (about 3½ juicy lemons)

Note: For this recipe you'll need a 16-ounce/240 ml sealable canning jar, sterilized with boiling water.

DIRECTIONS

Preheat a sous vide water bath to 167°F/75°C.

Whisk all of the ingredients together in a bowl and then pour into a resealable bag. Seal using the displacement method (see page 14), clip the bag to the side of the preheated water bath, and cook for 1 hour.

Remove the bag from the water bath and transfer the mixture to the jar. Put the lid on the jar and give it a good shake. Plunge the jar into an ice bath for 5 to 10 minutes, ensuring that the water goes only as far as the bottom of the lid. Refrigerate for 6 hours or overnight.

Chia seeds are huge in the health food world, touted for their multitude of health benefits. High in fiber, protein, and omega-3 fatty acids, chia seeds are said to boost healthy skin, hair, and nails; improve digestive health; and even promote heart health. Many recipes make you wait overnight for chia seeds to expand naturally and form chia pudding, but sous vide accelerates the process, allowing you to enjoy a chia pudding in less than an hour and a half. Also, although this recipe is in the desserts section, it's just as good for breakfast.

CHIA PUDDING POTS

♨ 140°F/60°C | 🕐 1 HOUR 25 MINUTES | 🍴 SERVES 4

INGREDIENTS

¾ cup/120 g chia seeds, plus a little extra to garnish

4 cups (950 ml) coconut milk

2 tablespoons/30 ml honey

4 drops vanilla extract

1 cup (240 ml) mango purée (or chopped mango if you prefer)

2 tablespoons sliced coconut flesh or dried shredded coconut

DIRECTIONS

Preheat a sous vide water bath to 140°F/60°C.

Combine the chia seeds, coconut milk, honey, and vanilla in a resealable plastic bag. Seal using the displacement method (see page 14), clip the bag to the side of the preheated water bath, and cook for 1 hour 25 minutes.

Remove the bag from the water bath and divide the contents among 4 bowls. Top each dish with the mango and coconut, then sprinkle over some extra chia seeds for a bit of crunch.

The beauty of this dish is in the different textures, flavors, and temperatures of chilled mango, warm rice pudding, and crunchy coconut shreds. While cooking rice pudding sous vide doesn't shorten the cooking time of rice pudding, it does make the time go by faster because it's hassle free. Yes, this is a "set it and forget it" rice pudding! No endless stirring, turning the heat up and down, and tasting a million times to see whether the rice is cooked. I'll bet nobody will be able to tell the difference.

TROPICAL RICE PUDDING

⊹ 185°F/85°C | ⏱ 4 HOURS | 🍴 SERVES 4

INGREDIENTS

⅔ cup/66 g Arborio rice

2 cups/475 ml coconut milk, plus extra to serve

½ cup (120 ml) whole milk

⅓ cup/70 g firmly packed brown sugar

1 fresh kaffir lime leaf or 2 dried

½ teaspoon/2½ ml vanilla extract

½ stalk lemongrass, bruised with the side of a knife

3 tablespoons shredded coconut, to serve

1 ripe mango, chilled

DIRECTIONS

Preheat a sous vide water bath to 185°F/85°C.

Combine the rice, coconut milk, whole milk, brown sugar, lime leaves, vanilla, and lemongrass in a bowl and stir to combine. Transfer the mixture to a resealable plastic bag. Seal using the displacement method (see page 14), clip the bag to the edge of the preheated water bath, and cook for 6 hours. For most rice varieties, this will be sufficient. However, I do recommend tasting the rice before taking it out of the bag. That way if your rice is still tough, you can continue cooking without much inconvenience.

Five minutes before the rice has finished cooking, chop the mango into ½-inch/1-cm cubes.

When the rice pudding has finished, tip it into a large bowl, removing the lemongrass and kaffir lime leaf. Add more warmed coconut milk if needed. Divide the pudding into bowls to serve, and pour warmed coconut milk on top. Arrange the mango cubes and shredded coconut on top and serve.

I've infused this creamy pourable custard with chai spices. The result is a wickedly delicious dessert topping that's just a little bit grown-up. If you manage not to finish it off by repeatedly "tasting" it on its own, it's fantastic poured over apple crumble, poached fruit (like the poached pears on page 236), or ice cream. It's also a natural for any fall-flavored desserts, thanks to the clove and cinnamon.

SPICED CHAI CUSTARD

🌡 176°F/80°C | ⏲ 25 MINUTES | 🍴 SERVES 4 TO 6

INGREDIENTS

2 cups/475 ml whole milk

2 cinnamon sticks

8 green cardamom pods

10 cloves

1 star anise

¼ teaspoon coriander seeds

1 teaspoon/5 ml vanilla extract

4 egg yolks

¾ cup/150 g sugar

DIRECTIONS

Preheat a sous vide water bath to 176°F/80°C.

Place the milk, cinnamon stick, cardamom pods, cloves, star anise, coriander seeds, and vanilla in a small saucepan and bring to a boil over medium-high heat. Remove from the heat, cover, and let steep for 10 minutes.

While it steeps, whisk together the egg yolks and sugar in a bowl until pale yellow.

Return the saucepan to medium-high heat and bring to a boil. Once the milk is boiling, strain out the solids, and pour the milk over the whisked egg yolk mixture a little at a time, whisking constantly. When the milk has been incorporated and the mixture is emulsified, return it to the saucepan. Add the vanilla and stir constantly until the mixture thickens and coats the back of a spoon, 2 to 3 minutes.

Pour the mixture into a resealable plastic bag. Seal using the displacement method (see page 14), clip the bag to the side of the preheated water bath, and cook for 25 minutes.

When the custard has finished cooking sous vide, you can either serve it immediately or chill it in the fridge until you're ready to serve. This custard can be served hot or cold.

Crème brûlée is the rarest of things: a classic dessert that always delivers with a wow factor. Cracking through that hardened caramelized sugar top to reveal a gooey interior is just so satisfying! As with most sous vide dishes, the benefit of using sous vide is precision and the ability to "set and forget" the brûlée as opposed to babysitting your food.

VANILLA CRÈME BRÛLÉE

🌡 176°F/80°C | ⏱ 25 MINUTES | 🍴 SERVES 4

INGREDIENTS

¼ cup/50 g sugar

5 egg yolks

2 cups/475 ml heavy cream

1 teaspoon/5 ml vanilla extract

2 tablespoons/23 g firmly packed brown sugar

2 tablespoons/25 g granulated sugar

Note: For this recipe you'll need 4 ramekins.

Note: If you want to get more adventurous, infuse the cream with 1½ tablespoons of culinary lavender. Strain it before whisking with the egg and sugar.

DIRECTIONS

Preheat a sous vide water bath to 176°F/80°C.

Whisk the sugar and egg yolks together in a large bowl until pale yellow.

Bring the cream to a boil in a small saucepan over medium-high heat. Once the cream begins to boil (but is not yet at a rolling, vigorous boil), remove it from the heat and slowly pour it over the whisked egg yolk mixture, whisking constantly. When the cream has been incorporated and the mixture is emulsified, return the mixture to the saucepan, add the vanilla, and stir constantly until the mixture thickens and coats the back of a spoon, 2 to 3 minutes. Pour the mixture into a resealable plastic bag. Seal using the displacement method (see page 14), clip the bag to the edge of the preheated water bath, and cook for 25 minutes.

Remove the bag from the water bath and divide the mixture among 4 ramekins, giving them a gentle jiggle to shake excess air out, and leave them on the countertop for 20 minutes. This serves a dual purpose: first, it allows the liquid to cool slightly before you put it in the fridge. Second, it lets bubbles escape for a smoother texture. Transfer the ramekins to the fridge for at least 2 hours or for up to 3 days.

Take the ramekins out of the fridge at least 30 minutes before serving. In a small bowl, combine the brown sugar and granulated sugar and stir to blend. Sprinkle each crème brûlée with the sugar mixture. Torch with a steady and gentle motion until caramelized.

Sometimes it can feel that it's hard to find a healthy drink that actually tastes great, especially when you're on the run. This is for everyone out there who loves flavored water without added sugar. These are simple, healthy, and definitely delicious! I've suggested berry, apple, and lemongrass, but feel free to get creative and use your favorite fruits or flavorings.

INFUSED WATER

🌡 167°F/75°C | ⏱ 4 HOURS | 🍴 SERVES 4

INGREDIENTS

BERRY WATER

4 cups/950 ml water

2 cups/140 g strawberries/
blueberries/blackberries

APPLE WATER

4 cups/950 ml water

2 apples, cored and thinly
sliced

LEMONGRASS WATER

4 cups/950 ml water

8 stalks lemongrass,
end trimmed

Note: If you prefer a sweeter beverage, you can add sugar syrup to taste.

DIRECTIONS

Preheat a sous vide water bath to 167°F/75°C.

Place half of the water and flavorings into one resealable plastic bag, and the other half into another. Seal using the displacement method (see page 14), clip the bags to the side of the preheated water bath, and cook for 4 hours.

After 4 hours, or when the flavor has developed to your desired strength, transfer the resealable plastic bags to an ice water bath for 5 to 10 minutes. Strain the solids out of the liquid with a wire mesh sieve and chill the flavored water in the fridge overnight or for up to 3 days.

Drink chilled, or over ice with garnishes.

We'll start the alcohol infusions with vodka because it's the most versatile spirit. It provides a neutral base for both delicate and more intense flavorings. Infusing vodka the regular way, at room temperature, usually takes from 3 to 7 days. With sous vide, you can do it in just a few hours!

By experimenting with different ingredients for different amounts of time, you'll be able to create a wide variety of flavors, from sipping vodka with just a subtle hint of flavor to strongly flavored vodka that's meant to shine through in a complex cocktail. Since vodka doesn't have much flavor on its own, there's less of a risk of creating clashing flavors than there is with rum or other spirits with more character.

INFUSED VODKA

Vanilla vodka is a classic bar staple, and with good reason, since it plays well with a variety of cocktail flavors, from espresso and chocolate to tropical fruits and orange. I've found you don't need long to get a full-flavored vanilla vodka, so the time on this one is just 2 hours.

Vanilla Vodka

🌡 135°F/57°C | ⏱ 2 HOURS | 🍴 MAKES 1 CUP

INGREDIENTS

1 cup/240 ml vodka

1 vanilla bean, split lengthwise

DIRECTIONS

Preheat a sous vide water bath to 135°F/57°C.

Combine the vodka and vanilla in a resealable plastic bag. Seal using the displacement method (see page 14), clip the bag to the edge of the preheated water bath, and cook for 2 hours.

After 2 hours, plunge the bag into an ice water bath for 5 to 10 minutes. Strain the liquid (discarding the vanilla bean) and transfer to a clean bottle or jar. Store in the fridge until ready to use.

This vodka is fantastic with Asian flavors, such as lychee, and ideal as an accompaniment to an Asian meal. The lemongrass and ginger take a while to really infuse, hence the longer sous vide time.

Chile, Ginger, and Lemongrass Vodka

🌡 135°F/57°C | ⏱ 5 HOURS | 🍴 MAKES 1 CUP

INGREDIENTS

1 cup/240 ml vodka

⅓ cup/75 g sliced ginger

1 or 2 small fresh red chiles, seeded and halved

1 stalk lemongrass, bruised with the side of a knife

DIRECTIONS

Preheat a sous vide water bath to 135°F/57°C.

Combine the vodka, ginger, chiles, and lemongrass in a resealable plastic bag. Seal using the displacement method (see page 14), clip the bag to the side of the preheated water bath, and cook for 5 hours. Plunge the bag into an ice water bath for 5 to 10 minutes. Strain the liquid (discarding the solids) and transfer to a clean bottle or jar. Store in the fridge until ready to use.

Unlike the other vodka recipes, this is a vodka-based infusion that's meant to be sipped on its own, rather than mixed in a cocktail. Be sure to cool the sugar water and the vodka all the way to serving temperature if you plan to go straight from infusing to sipping without a rest in the fridge.

Limoncello Vodka

🌡 135°F/57°C | ⏲ 2 HOURS | 🍴 MAKES 1⅔ CUPS

INGREDIENTS

4 lemons (organic, if possible)

1 cup/240 ml vodka

⅔ cup/160 ml water

½ cup/100 g sugar

DIRECTIONS

Preheat a sous vide water bath to 135°F/57°C.

Wash the lemons well in warm water and remove the peel with a peeler, making sure not to remove much of the white pith. Combine the vodka and lemon zest in a resealable plastic bag. Seal using the displacement method (see page 14), clip the bag to the side of the preheated water bath, and cook for 2 hours.

Meanwhile, bring the water to a boil in a small pot over medium-high heat. Remove the pot from the heat, add the sugar, and stir until it is completely dissolved. Cover the pot and set aside. If you'd like, you can place the pot in the fridge or freezer to bring down the temperature even further once the pot is cool enough.

When the vodka has finished cooking sous vide, remove the resealable plastic bag from the water bath and plunge it into an ice water bath for 5 to 10 minutes. Once the mixture is cool to the touch, squeeze the lemon peel pieces a bit through the bag, then open the bag and strain the vodka. Discard the peel. Add the infused vodka to the sugar syrup and stir to combine. Transfer to a sterilized bottle or jar. Store in the fridge until it's cool enough to serve.

Rum is a spirit that takes on flavors exceptionally well. Although you can easily find flavored rum, it's so much more satisfying to make it yourself! That way, you can avoid those dreaded fake flavors and control the strength (and quality) of what you're infusing. The recipes that follow are built around classic rum combinations, but feel free to experiment with other infusions as well.

INFUSED RUM

Homemade spiced rum is so much better than the store-bought stuff, though it may take some trial and error for you to hit on your magic spice combination. My favorite combination includes vanilla, cloves, cinnamon, peppercorns, star anise, and orange peel. Why not start here and see what you like (or want to remove for next time)?

Spiced Rum

🌡 135°F/57°C | 🕐 2½ HOURS | 🍴 MAKES 1 (375 ML) BOTTLE

INGREDIENTS

1 bottle/375 ml medium-bodied aged rum

1 vanilla bean, split lengthwise

2 whole cloves

1 cinnamon stick

2 whole black peppercorns

1 star anise

Peel of 1 orange, washed

DIRECTIONS

Preheat a sous vide water bath to 135°F/57°C.

Put all of the ingredients into a resealable plastic bag. Seal using the displacement method (see page 14), clip the bag to the side of the preheated water bath, and cook for 2½ hours. Remove the bag from the water bath and cool in an ice water bath for 5 to 10 minutes. Massage the solid ingredients through the bag, then strain out the solids and discard. I recommend pouring it right back into the bottle, then storing it in the fridge.

Personally, I can't stand the taste of Malibu rum (to each their own . . .), so if you're the same, don't think this tastes similar; it doesn't, at all! This tastes like real coconut (because that's what it's made with) and is fantastic in tropical cocktails. Malibu rum, eat your heart out!

Coconut Rum

🌡 135°F/57°C | ⏲ 2½ HOURS | 🍴 MAKES 1 (375 ML) BOTTLE

INGREDIENTS

1 whole, ripe coconut

1 bottle/375 ml white rum

DIRECTIONS

Preheat a sous vide water bath to 135°F/57°C.

Crack open your coconut and remove the meat, chopping it into small pieces (you're looking for around 10 ounces/285 g of coconut meat). Place the coconut meat into a resealable plastic bag along with the rum. Seal using the displacement method (see page 14), clip the bag to the side of the preheated water bath, and cook for 2½ hours. Remove the bag from the water bath and cool in an ice water bath for 5 to 10 minutes. Massage the coconut through the bag, then strain out the solids. I recommend pouring it right back into the bottle, then storing it in the fridge.

This mojito rum is the ideal mixer for—you guessed it—mojitos! But don't stop there. This minty, limey rum freshens up a Moscow mule, dark 'n stormy, Mai Tai, and planter's punch as well.

Mojito Rum

🌡 135°F/57°C | ⏲ 2½ HOURS | 🍴 MAKES 1 (375 ML) BOTTLE

INGREDIENTS

1 bottle/375 ml white rum

10 fresh mint leaves

Peel of 1 lime, washed

DIRECTIONS

Preheat a sous vide water bath to 135°F/57°C.

Put the rum, mint leaves, and lime peel into a resealable plastic bag. Seal using the displacement method (see page 14), clip the bag to the side of the preheated water bath, and cook for 2½ hours. Remove the bag from the water bath and massage the solid ingredients through the bag, then strain out the solids and discard. I recommend pouring it right back into the bottle, then storing it in the fridge.

Mulled wine is a Christmas classic, but there's no reason that it needs to be confined to the holidays! Spiced, sweet, heady, and satisfying, mulled wine is the boozy equivalent of comfort food. Although traditionally served hot, it's equally enjoyable sipped the next day after it has been chilled.

MULLED WINE

❄ 156°F/69°C | 🕐 3 HOURS | 🍴 SERVES 6 TO 8

Photo on following page.

INGREDIENTS

1 bottle/750 ml red wine
(Chianti or Cabernet
Sauvignon work well)

1 cup/240 ml orange juice
(freshly squeezed, if possible)

Peel of ½ orange

Peel of ½ lemon

1 cinnamon stick

¾ cup/150 g sugar

1 bay leaf

4 cloves

1 star anise

1 vanilla pod, split lengthwise

DIRECTIONS

Preheat a sous vide water bath to 156°F/69°C.

Combine all of the ingredients in a large bowl. Divide the mixture into 2 large resealable plastic bags. Seal using the displacement method (see page 14), clip the bag to the side of the preheated water bath, and cook for 3 hours.

Remove the bag from the water bath and strain the wine directly into a large serving bowl, discarding the solids, and then ladle into glasses to serve. You can also strain into a medium-size pot and reheat gently on the stove when it's time to serve.

A cup of spiced hot cider on a winter's day warms you through in the most satisfying way. In the warmer months, this drink is great chilled. Just allow it to cool first, then refrigerate it and serve over ice. You can also make a nonalcoholic version for the kids using apple juice or apple cider.

SPICED HOT CIDER

✱ 156°F/69°C | ⏱ 2 HOURS | ✗ SERVES 4

INGREDIENTS

2 cups/475 ml hard apple cider

1 cinnamon stick

1 tablespoon/15 ml maple syrup

3 whole black peppercorns

¼ cup/60 ml orange juice (freshly squeezed or very good quality if store bought)

DIRECTIONS

Preheat a sous vide water bath to 156°F/69°C.

Combine all of the ingredients in a resealable plastic bag. Seal using the displacement method (see page 14), clip the bag to the side of the preheated water bath, and cook for 3 hours. Remove the bag from the water bath and strain the contents into a large measuring cup, discarding the solids. If you want to serve the cider on the hotter side, microwave until the cider is about 190°F. Then pour into serving glasses, such as small teacups.

These oils may infuse quickly, but they are no half-strength shortcut: you get lots of flavor, be it of chile, rosemary, or garlic. The oils actually transform in color and gain huge aroma as well as a change in flavor. They're great drizzled over foods, stirred into soups, and you can even use them to stir-fry! I absolutely love using them for frying because they add an earthy depth of flavor to many dishes. And the best part? You don't have to wait days for the flavors to infuse! In just 3 hours you can get flavor-packed oils that are ready to drizzle, pour, or sizzle.

INFUSED OILS

§* 167°F/75°C | ⏱ 3 HOURS | ✗ MAKES 1½ CUPS/350 ML

Garlic oil is known for being delicious, but did you know it's also widely recognized for its antifungal and anti-inflammatory properties, as well as for fighting many skin conditions? While I can't vouch for those properties, but I can confirm it's delicious!

Garlic Oil

INGREDIENTS

1½ cups/350 ml of oil (see Note)

8 medium/large garlic cloves, each chopped into 4 pieces

DIRECTIONS

Preheat a sous vide water bath to 167°F/75°C.

Put all of the ingredients for the oil you choose into a resealable plastic bag. Seal using the displacement method (see page 14), clip the bag to the side of the preheated water bath, and cook for 3 hours. Remove the bag from the water bath, strain the oil to remove any solids, and transfer the oil to jars. Store the oil in the fridge. If the oil solidifies, warm it back up before serving.

This Asian-inspired chile oil has complex flavors that take it to another level of amazing. The Sichuan peppercorns warm your palate in a way that you'll never experience with other chile peppers. The star anise and cinnamon are supporting players, which help round it out.

Earthy Chile Oil

INGREDIENTS

1½ cups/350 ml vegetable or peanut oil

8 small red chiles, halved

3 star anise

1 tablespoon Sichuan peppercorns

2 tablespoons/12 g red pepper flakes

1 cinnamon stick

1 tablespoon/15 ml sesame oil (optional)

Note: If you're using these mainly for salad dressings, I recommend that you use olive oil. However, if you'll be using these oils for cooking, then vegetable oil is a better choice.

*Any chile lover knows the beauty of this oil.
Don't think of it as an Asian condiment, as
it is just as wonderful with pizza and pasta.*

Basic Chile Oil

INGREDIENTS

1½ cups/350 ml vegetable or peanut oil

8 to 10 small red chiles, halved

2 tablespoons/12 g red pepper flakes

*As you'd expect, this rosemary oil—as well
as the garlic oil (opposite)—are fantastic
for dipping bread. However, I've come to
rely on them for something else: homemade
salad dressing. By infusing some of the
flavors right into the oil, it makes for a
more complex dressing.*

Rosemary Oil

INGREDIENTS

1½ cups/350 ml oil (see Note)

8 sprigs rosemary

Olives are an all-time favorite appetizer straight out of the jar, but warmed olives spiked with seasonings are on another level. Although you might think tapas restaurants hold the secret to these addictive olives, you can actually make them yourself with sous vide. The heat will infuse the olives over just a few hours and the sealed bag means your olives won't lose precious moisture. If you want to make this recipe more cost-effective, you can substitute vegetable oil for the olive oil—it's actually very hard to tell the difference.

SPEED-MARINATED OLIVES

🌡 185°F/85°C | ⏲ 4 HOURS | 🍴 MAKES 1½ CUPS/350 ML

INGREDIENTS

ROSEMARY AND GARLIC OLIVES

1½ cups/150 g mixed black and green olives

1 cup/240 ml olive oil

4 sprigs rosemary

8 garlic cloves, halved

SPICY GARLIC OLIVES

1½ cups/150 g mixed black and green olives

1 cup/240 ml olive oil

10 small red chiles, roughly chopped

10 garlic cloves, halved

DIRECTIONS

Preheat a sous vide water bath to 185°F/85°C.

Place the olives in a resealable plastic bag with the oil and seasonings of your choice. Seal using the displacement method (see page 14), clip the bag to the side of the preheated water bath, and cook for 4 hours.

After 4 hours, you can serve the olives immediately or transfer them to a jar, pouring in as much of the flavorings and oil as will fit. Store the olives in the fridge and reheat gently over low heat on the stove or in the microwave before serving.

Your run-of-the-mill herb butter would simply have you melt butter, combine it with some herbs and flavorings, and then let it solidify in the fridge again. This butter takes the whole process to the next level. Instead of simply combining the butter with stuff, you're actually infusing the butter itself with the flavorings.

With so many uses, infused butter is handy to have in the fridge: it can start a meal with style when paired with a crusty loaf; a pat is one of the tastiest ways to finish a steak; and it can liven up asparagus, corn on the cob, or other hot vegetables. You can even use it to fry steaks and other meat.

INFUSED BUTTER

🌡 167°F/75°C | 🕐 1 TO 3 HOURS | 🍴 MAKES ½ CUP/113 G

INGREDIENTS

GARLIC BUTTER

8 tablespoons/113 g salted butter

1 tablespoon/9 g finely chopped garlic

1 teaspoon/5 g garlic powder

¼ cup/25 g finely grated Parmesan cheese

Salt and black pepper to taste

HERB BUTTER

8 tablespoons/113 g salted butter

1 tablespoon/6 g finely chopped fresh parsley

1 tablespoon/6 g finely chopped fresh chives

1 tablespoon/9 g finely chopped garlic

1 sprig fresh rosemary

Salt and black pepper to taste

TRUFFLE BUTTER

8 tablespoons/113 g salted butter

2 teaspoons/10 ml truffle oil

Salt to taste

DIRECTIONS

Preheat a sous vide water bath to 167°F/75°C.

Place the butter and the seasonings of your choice into a resealable bag. Seal using the displacement method (see page 14) and clip the bag to the side of the preheated water bath. For the Garlic Butter and the Herb Butter, cook sous vide for 3 hours to infuse. For the Truffle Butter, cook sous vide for just 1 hour to infuse.

Remove the bag from the water bath and give the contents a good stir. Plunge the bag into an ice water bath for 5 to 10 minutes to cool, then transfer the bag to the fridge for about 3 hours, or until the butter has firmed up enough to work with but is still soft and malleable.

Lay out about 12 inches/30 cm of plastic wrap on the counter and transfer the butter to the center of the plastic. Roll up the plastic around the butter and form the butter into a sausage shape, twisting the ends tight and tying in knots. Return the butter to the fridge and let it finish firming up. Store the butter in the fridge until you're ready to use it.

PRESERVED CITRUS

🌡 185°F/95°C | ⏲ 4½ HOURS | 🍴 MAKES ONE 16-OUNCE/475 ML CANNING JAR

INGREDIENTS

LEMONS

1½ tablespoons sea salt (not table salt), plus ample extra to rub into the lemon wedges

5 unwaxed, organic lemons, washed well, each cut into 8 wedges

½ cup/120 ml freshly squeezed lemon juice (about 1 juicy lemon)

1 bay leaf

1 cup/240 ml just-boiled water

LIMES

1½ tablespoons sea salt (not table salt), plus ample extra to rub into the lime wedges

7 unwaxed, organic limes, washed well, each cut into 8 wedges

¼ cup/60 ml freshly squeezed lemon juice

¼ cup/60 ml freshly squeezed lime juice

1 bay leaf

1 cup/240 ml just-boiled water

ORANGES

3 tablespoons/36 g sea salt (not table salt), plus ample extra to rub into the orange wedges

4 unwaxed, organic oranges, washed well, each cut into 8 wedges

¼ cup/60 ml freshly squeezed lemon juice

¼ cup/60 ml freshly squeezed orange juice

1 bay leaf

1 cup/240 ml just-boiled water

Note: For these recipes you'll need a 16-ounce/475 ml canning jar, sterilized for 10 minutes in boiling water.

DIRECTIONS

Preheat a sous vide water bath to 185°F/95°C; it helps to cover the water bath with foil (if it doesn't already have a lid) to help the water heat up faster.

In a large bowl, rub a generous amount of salt onto the surfaces of the citrus wedges. Transfer the wedges to a resealable bag, and add the juice, sea salt, bay leaf and just-boiled water called for in your recipe. Massage the contents of the bag with your hands through the plastic for a few seconds. Seal the bag using the displacement method (see page 14), clip the bag to the side of the preheated water bath, and cook for 4½ hours.

Remove the bag from the water bath and plunge into an ice water bath. Once cool enough to handle, transfer the solid contents to a canning jar, and then pour in as much liquid as will fit. Store in the fridge for 6 hours or overnight. They will last in the fridge for weeks.

To use your preserved citrus fruit, rinse the wedges well to remove excess salt. Discard the flesh and either cut the rind into strips or leave in chunks.

Once you have preserved citrus in your fridge, you'll find uses for it in all sorts of dishes. It goes well on toast and in salads, dressings, salsas, and dips, and is a great seasoning for lamb. I even eat the citrus alone. And I don't stop at preserved lemons either—I've found preserved limes and oranges are every bit as tasty.

Pickled radishes are a wonderful addition to your fridge. Not only are they a fantastic snack, but also they can bring a big pop of flavor to your salads. These are cooked for long enough that the radishes have softened, but they still have a good amount of crunch. Depending on how thick you like to slice your radishes, you may want to reduce or increase the cooking time (the thicker the slice, the longer the cooking time).

PICKLED RADISHES WITH PEPPERCORNS AND MUSTARD SEEDS

🌡 185°F/85°C | ⏱ 30 MINUTES | 🍴 MAKES ABOUT 1 CUP/240 ML

INGREDIENTS

4 large/medium radishes or 8 small, stems trimmed, thinly sliced

⅔ cup/160 ml white vinegar

⅔ cup/160 ml filtered water

2 tablespoons/25 g sugar

2 teaspoons/13 g salt

½ teaspoon mustard seeds

½ teaspoon black peppercorns

½ to 1 teaspoon/1 to 2 g red pepper flakes (optional, depending on how much you like spice)

Note: For this recipe you'll need an 8-ounce/240 ml sealable canning jar, sterilized with boiling water.

DIRECTIONS

Combine all of the ingredients in a resealable plastic bag. Shake and massage the contents with your hands to make sure all of the ingredients are well combined. If you want to give the radishes a bit of extra pickling time, you can do this before you turn on your sous vide machine to give the radishes some extra time in the liquid.

Preheat a sous vide machine to 185°F/85°C; it helps to cover the water bath with tin foil (if it doesn't already have a lid) to help the water heat up faster.

Seal the bag using the displacement method (see page 14), clip the bag to the side of the preheated water bath, and cook for 30 minutes.

Remove the bag from the water bath and plunge the bag into an ice bath for 5 to 10 minutes, or until cool. Transfer the contents of the bag to a jar and store in the fridge. They're ready to eat as soon as they're chilled, but will get even better in the fridge over the following days. These should last a few weeks in the fridge.

INDEX

RESOURCES

Websites

ChefSteps

www.chefsteps.com

This site is ideal for people who are looking for high-tech cooking information. The recipes aren't always the easiest to execute, but they focus on getting great results. As is evident in the website's forums, it's used by both chefs and home cooks.

Serious Eats

www.seriouseats.com

This is a useful website and blog for food enthusiasts. J. Kenji López-Alt's column, The Food Lab, has lots of great information about sous vide cooking. It's where Kenji, the former editor at *Cook's Illustrated* magazine and author of *The Food Lab: Better Home Cooking Through Science*, tests out all sorts of techniques and recipes and documents his findings.

Modernist Cooking Made Easy

www.modernistcookingmadeeasy.com

This site has hundreds of sous vide recipes, as well as some handy basic guides. It's owned by Jason Logsdon, who has also written a number of books on sous vide cooking.

Books

Under Pressure
THOMAS KELLER

If you want to look at some really sexy sous vide photos, this book is where it's at. But be warned, the recipes are pretty advanced. Many are downright daunting for the average home cook, but it's great to see what's possible with sous vide.

Cooking for Geeks
JEFF POTTER

This book looks at all manner of geeky food techniques, not just sous vide. It's great for those who want to know the science behind modern cooking techniques (e.g., hydrocolloids, Maillard reactions, and more).

Modernist Cuisine: The Art and Science of Cooking
NATHAN MYHRVOLD

Don't let the author line fool you: this set of books is actually the accumulated efforts of a team of scientists, research and development chefs, and a full editorial team. The idea behind it is for the book to be the bible of modernist cuisine, which includes sous vide. If you're a food science geek and are serious about the modernist techniques, you may want to invest in this one—or at least read as much as you can at the library or a local bookstore. At $500, it's not an impulse buy!

Sous Vide for the Home Cook
DOUGLAS E. BALDWIN

One of the main problems with the first few sous vide books that came out was that they were too advanced for the average home cook. This book dials down the fancy techniques and dishes out more than 200 recipes in the process.

ABOUT THE AUTHOR

Christina Wylie is an award-winning food writer, food stylist, journalist, and radio host. She is the founder and editor of the online lifestyle magazine *The GAB*, where she leads a team of sixty writers. She has worked as a recipe developer and blogger for Anova Culinary and her recipes and writing have been featured worldwide, including in *The Times*, *The Sunday Times*<M>, various Time Out publications, *Traveler's Digest*, *Wining & Dining*, and many more.

A lifelong globetrotter, Christina was on the founding board of the charity initiative Project Gen Z and the Dare to Dream workshops, which teach orphaned children in Cambodia entrepreneurial skills. She is currently launching two new food and culture magazines, as well as her first restaurant, Bootlegger.